MW01505682

Looking
FOR
God

DONNA VANLIERE

HARVEST HOUSE PUBLISHERS
EUGENE, OREGON

Unless otherwise indicated, all Scripture verses are taken from the *Holy Bible*, New Living Translation, copyright © 1996, 2004, 2015 by Tyndale House Foundation. Used with permission of Tyndale House Publishers, Carol Stream, Illinois 60188. All rights reserved.

Other Bible translations used are credited in the back of the book.

Cover design by Faceout Studio, Addie Lutzo
Cover images © Bibleboxone / Shutterstock
Interior design by Janelle Coury
Interior images © Natalllenka.m, true north 72, steshs / Shutterstock

For bulk, special sales, or ministry purchases, please call 1-800-547-8979.
Email: CustomerService@hhpbooks.com

This book includes accounts in which the author has changed people's names in order to protect their privacy.

LOOKING FOR GOD

Copyright © 2026 by Donna VanLiere
Published by Harvest House Publishers
Eugene, Oregon 97408
www.harvesthousepublishers.com

ISBN 978-0-7369-9213-8 (hardcover)
ISBN 978-0-7369-9214-5 (eBook)

Library of Congress Control Number: 2025936301

Printed in China

25 26 27 28 29 30 31 32 33 34 / DC / 10 9 8 7 6 5 4 3 2 1

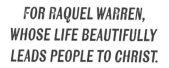

FOR RAQUEL WARREN,
WHOSE LIFE BEAUTIFULLY
LEADS PEOPLE TO CHRIST.

Also by
Donna VanLiere

DONNA VANLIERE
NEW YORK TIMES BESTSELLING AUTHOR OF
THE CHRISTMAS SHOES

Looking
FOR
Christmas

A SEARCH FOR THE
JOY AND HOPE
OF THE NATIVITY

Contents

ONE

Looking at God's Heart for You

I glanced down at my phone and saw that Nicole Fischer, a woman in our church, was texting. I knew the backstory of this beautiful woman, and how she and her husband, Travis, had been walking through a terrible illness he had suffered over the last few years. In his health journey, Travis had been through multiple procedures and surgeries and was on several medications. They had small children at home, and the stress had caught up with Nicole. She said she was dealing with terrible anxiety and asked if it was possible to meet me at the church so I could pray for her.

I contacted another woman from our prayer group who was available at that time, and we quickly made our way to the church. As I drove, I asked God to touch Nicole's heart in a way that she could understand. Immediately, the words "The Lord your God is with you…He will rejoice over you with singing" came to mind. I knew that came from a verse in Zephaniah, but I couldn't remember exactly where. I sensed that God wanted Nicole to know that He was not only with her but was rejoicing over her with singing, just like a parent comforting a child and holding her as she drifts off to sleep.

When I got to the church, I quickly looked up the verse on my phone and found it was Zephaniah 3:17: "The LORD your God is with you, the Mighty Warrior who saves. He will take great delight in you; in his love he will no longer rebuke you, but will rejoice over you with singing" (NIV).

The three of us slipped into a room and sat down, and I told Nicole about the verse that came to my mind. When I read it, tears began to stream down her face. She said, "That is my favorite verse in the Bible! It means so much to me that a friend of mine created a painting with those words, and I have it hanging in my home." She wiped the tears from her eyes and said, "God knew I needed to hear that. I needed to know that He sees me and He's fighting for me—for my family."

You might call that a coincidence, but there are more than 31,000 verses in the Bible, and the verse that came to my mind was the *one* verse that meant the most to Nicole. She was looking for God in the middle of the fallout of stress and anxiety from dealing for so long with Travis's health issues, and God, in His goodness, gave her a personal message from His heart to hers. He may not touch you exactly like that, but God wants to reach you with His love in a way that you can understand.

THE DOOR OF A BROTHEL

When I told my husband, Troy, that I was writing a book titled *Looking for God*, he asked, "Are you going to use that quote about knocking on the door of a brothel?" I wasn't familiar with the quote and was intrigued, so I looked it up. I discovered that in 1945, a Scottish writer named Bruce Marshall wrote a novel entitled *The World, the Flesh and Father Smith*. Within the story, the character of Father Smith says, in part, that "the young man who rings the bell at the brothel is unconsciously looking for God."[1]

Father Smith was saying that a young man who does that is seeking immediate pleasure, but ultimately, he is looking for love. Ecclesiastes 3:11 says that God "has planted eternity in the human heart." Each of us has, in our hearts, a sense of eternity, which was put there by God. But all of us also have our own "brothel" doors that we are knocking on because we're searching for something to fill that eternity-shaped hole inside of us. Either we will fill it with God and His truth and love, or we will pound on the door of money, power, sex, sports, fame, women, men, work, education, gangs, social media, exercise, gambling, gaming, cosmetic procedures, intimacy, significance, success, knowledge, pleasure, possessions, porn, or position as we look unconsciously for God.

You may say that you aren't knocking on any "brothel" door, but what if you are? What if your search for love and connection in this world has left you empty because you have yet to knock on God's door and know His real love in an unreal world? The Bible tells us that "God is love" (1 John 4:8), so shouldn't that satisfy us? Why do we keep knocking on brothel doors?

YOU WERE CREATED ON PURPOSE

My friend Carmen hosts a radio program called *The Reconnect with Carmen LaBerge*. We were chatting one day about why we continue to knock on doors in life that ultimately will never satisfy. Carmen is one of the smartest and wisest people I know, and she said, "People can't get their mind around the idea that God made them on purpose. They don't believe they are created, so why look for a creator? It's an endless cycle of folly as they continue to make and remake themselves into something else, but they can never achieve what they are imagining. It's exhausting and makes people despair."

Carmen is absolutely right. Why would anyone ever knock on God's door if they don't believe that God loves them and that He created them? Instead, they will easily get caught up in the endless cycle of folly that leads to knocking on one "brothel" door after another. A.W. Tozer (1897–1963) said,

> …the enemy of man's soul has mugged humanity, robbing them of their identity, men and women wander around in a spiritual and moral fog, not knowing who they are, what they are, or where they are going. People do not know why they are here…and do not know their purpose in life, why they were created, or what they are sent to do. Consequently, lives are filled with confusion, reaching out for any explanation; hence the proliferation of religions in our world. Religion only addresses man's external condition, not his internal confusion.[2]

Religion is our attempt to find God. It's also legalistic: Do this or that, or take that action, and it is easy yet exhausting to get caught on that hamster wheel. However, when we look for a relationship with God, we are met with His grace and find hope and peace. We will not find our purpose on the hamster wheel of religion, but rather, in a true relationship with the God who loves us.

How can you believe that God loves you or that you were created on purpose, or that you even have a purpose, if you grew up in a home where you heard the opposite? Or if you have lived with a spouse or someone else who would rather tear you down than build you up?

Throughout the Bible, we are told truths like these:

> The LORD will fulfill his purpose for me (Psalm 138:8 ESV).

> Those who love God...are called according to his purpose (Romans 8:28).

> You made all the delicate, inner parts of my body and knit me together in my mother's womb. Thank you for making me so wonderfully complex! (Psalm 139:13-14).

> God created human beings in his own image. In the image of God he created them; male and female he created them (Genesis 1:27).

> For through him God created everything in the heavenly realms and on earth...Everything was created through him and for him (Colossians 1:16).

> You created all things, and they exist because *you created what you pleased* (Revelation 4:11, emphasis added).

It pleased God to create you, but you have to decide whether you believe that. Henri Nouwen (1932–1996) said,

> The greatest spiritual battle begins—and never ends—with the reclaiming of our chosenness. Long before any human being saw us, we are seen by God's loving eyes. Long before anyone heard us cry or laugh, we are heard by our God who is all ears for us. Long before any person spoke to us in this world, we are spoken to by the voice of eternal love.[3]

God loved you way before anyone knew you even existed. When you talk to Him, your voice is heard in heaven! You may feel that you have not had a voice in your current circumstances, but God loves to hear what you say, and bends down to listen to you (Psalm 116:2).

GOD IS SEEKING YOU

Again, God loves you so much that He created you on purpose and *for* a purpose! No one is a mistake, and no one is so lost that he can't be found. God created us to seek Him (Acts 17:27), and most remarkable of all is that God is seeking you! The Creator of this world says in Ezekiel 34:16, "I will search for my lost ones who strayed away, and I will bring them safely home again. I will bandage the injured and strengthen the weak." His Son, Jesus, says,

"The Son of Man came to seek and save those who are lost" (Luke 19:10). But what is "lost"?

In 2005, NFL quarterback Tom Brady sat down for an interview with *60 Minutes*. At that time, he had led the New England Patriots to a Super Bowl win three times (he went on to earn four more Super Bowl victories: three additional wins for the Patriots, and one for the Tampa Bay Buccaneers). In the interview he said, "Why do I have three Super Bowl rings and still think there's something greater out there for me?...I think, God, there's got to be something more than this...What else is there for me?"

Reporter Steve Kroft asked, "What's the answer?"

Brady replied, "I wish I knew. I wish I knew."[4]

That's a perfect definition of lost. Like Tom Brady, you may think there's got to be something more than this and you keep searching, diligently trying to find what you're looking for. There's a lostness we all experience—it's that place in our hearts where God has set eternity (Ecclesiastes 3:11), and in our search for that "something more," we fill up that hole in our heart with everything that's behind the brothel door.

Remember the young man who knocked on the brothel door? He was lost, searching for something to fill the eternity-shaped hole in him. He was searching for love, not knowing God alone can give the love that would fulfill him. Jesus came to Earth to make God's love known to those who are lost—those who don't have a relationship with Him.

You may be busy knocking on doors, but God Himself is knocking on yours. A.W. Tozer said, "Christian theology teaches the doctrine of prevenient grace, which briefly stated means this: that, before a man can seek God, God must first have sought the man. We pursue God, because, and only because, He has first put an urge within us that spurs us to the pursuit. 'No man can come to me,' said our Lord, 'except the Father, which had sent me draw him.'"[5]

Charles Spurgeon (1834–1892) said that God knocks on your door for your

> immediate and endless happiness…Do not, therefore, act as if you were not at home: do not turn a deaf ear, or a careless heart. I am asking nothing of you in the name of God or man. It is not my intent to make any requirement at your hands; but I come in God's name, to bring you a free gift, which it shall be to your present and eternal joy to receive. Open the door, and let my pleadings enter.[6]

As you read the pages of this book, remember Spurgeon's plea, and don't act as if you are not at home. Open the door to receive God's love.

YOU WERE CREATED TO SEEK GOD

Google has been doing their Year in Search project for 22 years, and according to the website, these year-in-review results have "provided a unique look into what we all cared about, what inspired us and intrigued us, all over the world." The search results for 2022 revealed, "Global search interest in 'how to change myself' and 'how to be better' reached an all-time high this year."[7]

But in the searches for "how to change myself" and "how to be better," I discovered there wasn't one faith-based website in the top 100 searches, but there were several porn sites listed. In the top 20 alone, there were four of them.[8] The Bible or God wasn't listed; there was absolutely nothing faith-based in the top 100 searches. At the time of this writing in 2025, Google processes roughly 9.5 million searches every minute. That's 13.7 billion searches a day.[9] Now let this sink in: In the nearly 14 billion searches a day, God was nowhere to be found in the top 100 searches. By this data, it appears that few people are looking for God. Jesus said, "I have come that they may have life and have it abundantly" (John 10:10 NASB). But very few want to google that.

In the pages of this book, I hope to provide you with some of the answers that don't make the top 100 searches on Google. You may be someone who sporadically goes to church and believes in God, that He is up there somewhere, sitting in the clouds. You believe in God—great! But even the demons believe in God (James 2:19). There is a difference between believing *in* God and *believing God.*

When the prophet Jonah told the Ninevites that God was going to destroy them unless they repented, the Bible says, "The Ninevites believed God" (Jonah 3:5 NIV). What you believe about God matters. The Ninevites believed His word. They believed what He said and that He would do what He said. They didn't parse down the message to make it more palatable. They believed God and repented (they turned away from their sin that separated them from God).

Jesus said to His disciples, who had seen Him in person, "Blessed are those who believe without seeing me" (John 20:29). Throughout this book, ask yourself if you actually *believe God.* Do you believe He is who He says He is? Do you believe what He says in His Word? Do you believe what He says about His love for you?

Or perhaps you are someone who is "satisfied in your belief that there is a God" and "are not expected thereafter to crave any further revelation of God to our souls… that if we have found Him, we need no more seek Him."[10] Maybe you have vague ideas about God. Perhaps you have believed the lies that He hates this group of people or that. You might possibly be a skeptic or an atheist who is searching for answers, and as you read this book, you may be prompted to reevaluate your position.

Or, maybe you have been hurt in church and you want nothing to do with God, but the very fact that you are still reading this sentence proves that deep within, you are still seeking Him. You may believe that only theologians, pastors, ministers, or seminary professors can teach you about God, but in Jesus' day, the members of the Sanhedrin (the Jewish legislative and judicial council) took note that common fishermen "with no special training" had been with Jesus (Acts 4:13). If someone walks with Jesus, he can lead you to God the Father at the gym, the grocery store, on the factory floor, around the water cooler, in a school hall, or within the pages of a book. No college or seminary degrees are required.

What may surprise you is that God created us to seek Him. Acts 17:27-28 says this about God's purpose for mankind: "His purpose was for the nations *to seek after God and perhaps feel their way toward him and find him*— though he is not far from any one of us. For in him we live and move and exist" (emphasis added). If there is something deep inside of you that is groping and striving toward something, I would suggest that you are *looking for God*, and Acts 17:27-28 says that God created you to do that!

If you're knocking on "brothel" doors to fill the void

within you, ease the pain, or silence the noise inside, would you be open to the possibility that ultimately, you're looking for something more, something deeper in the form of God's love? If so, then I encourage you to pray this simple prayer:

> *Father God, I am searching for answers and giving this a shot. Please open the door of my heart, mind, soul, and spirit to believe that You are who You say You are. In Jesus' name, amen.*

You may say that all of this God stuff is nonsense and make-believe. But what if you're wrong? Are you open to that possibility? What if this book is the beginning of faith in your life? Referencing Romans 10:17, Charles Spurgeon said, "Faith comes by hearing, and reading is a sort of hearing: faith may come to you while you are reading this book. Why not? O blessed Spirit of all grace, make it so!"[11]

TWO

Looking at the God Who Adopts You

I had to go to my brother's house to pick up something, and when I walked into the kitchen, I saw my mom sitting there. She pretended like she didn't see me; like I wasn't even there." The man wanted me to pray for him at the end of a church service at Place of Hope, an in-house alcohol and drug treatment center in Columbia, Tennessee. He was thirtysomething, didn't tell me his name, and had a hard time looking me in the eyes.

"When was the last time you saw her?" I asked.

He shrugged. "Eight or ten years, I guess. I haven't talked to her in at least twenty. She never wanted me. She can't stand me. So I left home when I was sixteen. That's when I became an addict, but I was already drinking before that to feel better about my life."

Mental abuse, a lack of love, and neglect create the

perfect storm for addiction. "Did she ever say anything to you that day?" I asked.

He shook his head. "No. She could've at least said that she never wanted to see me again. That would've been better than silence. I just picked up what I needed and left."

GOD DOES NOT ABANDON YOU

Like this man who spent his life battling addiction because he grew up in a home without love, you may have grown up feeling unwanted and unloved. You may still feel that way today. But God makes it clear that even before He formed you—and anything that is formed has to be molded and shaped by its creator—He knew you. God said in Jeremiah 1:5, "I knew you before I formed you in your mother's womb." While God spoke those words to the prophet Jeremiah, they are true about everyone He creates. David wrote in Psalm 139:16, "You saw me before I was born. Every day of my life was recorded in your book. Every moment was laid out before a single day had passed."

God saw you before you were born and wrote down every day of your life in His book. That's amazing! No other god has done that. You are supposed to be here. You have a purpose. Psalm 138:8 says that God will fulfill His purpose for you. Galatians 1:15 says that before you were born, God chose and called you by His marvelous grace. You may feel unwanted in this world, but before you took your first breath, God chose you and called you by His grace because He loves you. He's still calling you today.

Despite what this world has thrown at you, and despite the conditions you grew up in, please remember that God will never forget you. In Isaiah 49:15-16, God says, "Can a mother forget her nursing child? Can she feel no love for the child she has borne? But even if that were possible, I would not forget you! See, I have written your name on the palms of my hands." God created the earth, the sun, the moon, the stars, the sky, the land and the waters, vegetation, all the beasts of the fields, birds in the skies, and life within the waters. He created male and female, and He said that everything He created was very good. That was the beginning of all things. Your very existence is tied to the beginning of all things!

WE ARE GIVEN THE OPPORTUNITY TO BECOME CHILDREN OF GOD

The Bible tells us that "to all who believed him and accepted him, he gave the right to become children of God" (John 1:12). Amazingly, when we place our belief in Christ, we become part of God's family, and the Holy Spirit is sent to live in us. This invitation is extended to everyone.

Romans 8:14 talks about becoming part of God's family: "All who are led by the Spirit of God are children of

God." If we are led by the Spirit of God, we are a child of God. We are *all* God's creation, but not everyone is a child of God. The Bible clarifies that there are two distinct groups—1 John 3:10 says, "We can tell who are children of God and who are children of the devil. Anyone who does not live righteously and does not love other believers does not belong to God." When a person becomes a child of God, they receive God's Spirit and they are adopted as His children. God does this because of His love for us.

All three of my children are adopted. They did not choose to be adopted; Troy and I chose to adopt them before they were even born. Before we saw any photos of them, we were calling them our children. When we received photos of each one, we emailed those photos to family and friends, and said, "Here is a picture of our daughter, Gracie, in China," or "This is a photo of our daughter, Kate, who is waiting for us in China," or "We would like to introduce you to our son, David, who we will be bringing home from Guatemala in a few months!" Through adoption, we were grafted together as family. Before we ever held any of them, we loved them as our children.

God doesn't look at us as mere creatures, subjects, or slaves. We are His creation. And when we place our belief in Him through Jesus Christ, we are then adopted and called His children. Just like Troy and I decided to adopt our children before they were born, the Bible says God decided to adopt those who become His children. As Ephesians 1:5 says, "God decided in advance to adopt us into his own family by bringing us to himself through Jesus Christ. This is what he wanted to do, and it gave him great pleasure." This is made possible through belief in Jesus Christ. In my studies, I can't find where any other god adopts humans as their children.

CHOSEN BY GOD

Several years ago, we were on a cruise with friends. Throughout the week, when we ate dinner, we would pray first. We had the same server throughout the week, a kind thirtysomething man with a soft accent. As we were getting up from the table after our final dinner, our waiter ran up to me and my friend Terrie Carswell, and said, "I have seen you praying throughout the week. Could you please pray that God would accept me into His kingdom?"

Terrie replied, "You can pray that yourself. God loves you and gave His Son Jesus so that we could come to Him."

The man shook his head and said, "Oh, no! I can't do that. I need to get my life in order before I pray that. There are many things I must do."

Workers were bustling around us, and people were bumping into us as they were leaving the dining hall, but both Terrie and I wanted to help him understand. "No," I said. "You don't have to do anything with your life to call on God. In the Bible, He says, 'When you call, I will answer.' 'For everyone who calls on the name of the LORD will be saved'" (Romans 10:13).

"He gave us Jesus," Terrie said. "Who is the way to the Father. Just call on the name of Jesus and…"

"No, no, I can't do that," he said, cutting her off. "There's so much I must do! Please pray for me." He smiled and hurried off. Terrie and I both felt sad for him because, like so many people, he had gotten some bad intel about God. He thought he had to do more—to clean himself up and get his act together before he could come to God. He didn't realize that when God saves a person, it is "not because of the righteous things we [have] done, but because of his mercy" (Titus 3:5). We don't earn God's mercy; salvation is a free gift (Romans 6:23). Like the Ninevites in the story of Jonah, we must believe God and repent of the sin that separates us from Him. Repenting is feeling remorse for the sin in our life and then turning away from it and to God.

There are no verses in the Bible that say anything about getting your life together or dealing with your past before coming to God. God knew that sin would mar this world and our lives (sin entered the world through Adam and Eve in Genesis 3), and He would use Jesus to bring us to

Him. Jesus knew the time would come for Him to come to Earth and lay down His life for us. He did that while we were still sinners and enemies of God, not after we had cleaned ourselves up, or gotten our acts together:

> God showed his great love for us by sending Christ to die for us while we were still sinners. And since we have been made right in God's sight by the blood of Christ, he will certainly save us from God's condemnation. For since our friendship with God was restored by the death of his Son while we were still his enemies, we will certainly be saved through the life of his Son (Romans 5:8-10).

God planned you. God loves you. He knew that His Son would be despised here on Earth but planned to make our salvation possible through Jesus while we were still His enemy. Think about that! I wouldn't even want an enemy near me, let alone think about planning his salvation. And I certainly wouldn't throw my son into the midst of wolves who are out to devour him, but God's ways are not our ways.

And keep in mind that Jesus agreed to this plan. He knew beforehand what was going to happen to Him and He came for us anyway. Now that's love! You are loved. His love is far beyond our understanding. Ephesians 1:6 reminds us that our salvation is through His marvelous grace. Grace is unearned favor. You don't deserve it. I don't deserve it. None of us do. An enemy of God deserves judgment and condemnation, but through Jesus, we receive God's grace. You can't work toward and earn grace. You just receive it. On the cruise, our waiter could not wrap his mind around that. He thought he had to do more. That is what other religions want from you: do more. With Jesus, it's already done.

PERFECT LOVE

She sat with us at a small table at a local restaurant, and her face revealed her anguish. Erica was only in her early thirties but looked ten years older. "He left me and the baby and moved in with another woman and her children." There were no tears this time as there had been on previous occasions when her husband had been unfaithful. She simply sat there dismayed and feeling helpless. In their few years of marriage, I think she had lost count of how many times he had been unfaithful to her. Even though I always liked her husband, I thought many times that she was either crazy to stay in that mess of a marriage or a saint, and on this occasion, that same thought came to mind. Perhaps they both thought that having a child would help keep him from wandering. But now, over a year later, Erica would need help with her toddler as her husband took up residence in another woman's home.

"I would take him back," Erica said, looking at us. I didn't say anything, but I couldn't understand the love she had for him. Why would she even want him back after all that he had done to her? "I love him. I married him for life. I would take him back because I love him so much."

Adam and Eve knew perfect love in the garden of Eden. They lived in paradise, and all their needs were met. In the cool of the day, God walked with them. The Bible doesn't say that God spent time with the animals or marveled at the beauty of the garden. Rather, God was in fellowship with Adam and Eve. They had relationship with Him. Their purpose was shared by nothing else in all of God's creation. They were completely unique. Everything in the garden was in perfect harmony. They could go anywhere and do anything *except* they could not eat the fruit from the tree of the knowledge of good and evil (Genesis 2:17). That was their only condition for living in paradise.

But the serpent got into Eve's head by saying, "Did God really say you must not eat the fruit from any of the trees in the garden?" (Genesis 3:1). He told her that God didn't want her to eat from the tree of the knowledge of good and evil because if she ate the fruit, she would be like Him. Paul David Tripp says,

> Satan is not tempting Eve with a better menu than what God had provided. He is tempting her with *autonomy* and self-*sufficiency*. His

> pitch is "you can be like God." Genesis 3:6 says of the tree that Eve *wanted the wisdom it would give her.* She walked in relationship with God, so why wasn't his wisdom enough? What attracted Eve was not just wisdom, but *autonomous wisdom*, that is, wisdom that did not require reliance on, and submission to God.[1]

That lured her in. Ephesians 4:27 warns us, "Do not give the devil a foothold" (NIV), but Eve did, and Adam followed suit. They ate the fruit and God had to remove them from Eden, permanently blocking their way back in. Why did He do that? Because if they were permitted to live in Eden and eat from its fruit, it would mean that they would live forever in that fallen, rebellious, sinful state. The undeniable tragedy here is that Adam and Eve lost their purpose. They had walked with God and enjoyed Him and His creation, and then gave it up. "Hand-in-hand, they made their way out into the world, not knowing where they were going. Humanity still wanders in this moral and spiritual wilderness."[2] This was not the Father's choice; this was on Adam and Eve. The Father heart of God wanted them to live in paradise with Him, sheltered by His love, safety, and friendship. In the same way, the Father heart of God wanted Erica's husband to stay faithful within their marriage and raise their child together.

The earth belongs to the Lord (Psalm 24:1), but it was

given to Adam and Eve to enjoy. When they broke their covenant with God, Satan became ruler and god of this world (John 12:31; 14:30; 16:11; 2 Corinthians 4:4), and the prince of the power of the air (Ephesians 2:2). Because of the rebellion in Eden, there are now two kingdoms at work in this world: the kingdom of God and light, and the kingdom of Satan and darkness (Mark 1:14-15; Ephesians 5:8; Colossians 1:13). There has been a cosmic war since Satan deceived Eve and Adam in the garden. (Despite what many believe, Satan is a real being. He appears in the Bible from Genesis to Revelation and is called the father of lies, the devil, the ruler of demons, the evil one, the tempter, the accuser, a murderer, our adversary, and deceiver of the whole world, among other names [Matthew 4:1-3; 9:34; 13:19; John 8:44; 1 Peter 5:8; Revelation 12:9-10].) The kingdoms of light and darkness cannot coexist in peace. It's impossible. But God allows us to choose which kingdom we live in and serve. When we are not in the kingdom of God, we are an enemy of God (Romans 5:10). Our choice determines whether we are "children of God" or "children of the devil" (1 John 3:10).

GOD WANTS YOU BACK!

Here's the great part. We are human, and God knew that sin would get the best of us. From the point of banishment from Eden forward, the Father set in motion a plan of restoration. He wanted Adam and Eve back, just as Erica wanted her husband back. God wants all of humanity back from the grip of disorder, confusion, rebellion, disobedience, and hate. In other words, He loves us and wants to save us from a sin-soaked world. The only way He could do that was to provide a bridge from this world to the Father, and this is where Jesus, the Son of God, steps into humanity. The Bible tells us that Jesus came at just the right time. "When we were utterly helpless, Christ came at just the right time and died for us sinners" (Romans 5:6). (For a deeper look into Christ's perfectly timed entrance into the world, read *Looking for Christmas: A Search for the Joy and Hope of the Nativity*.)

Just like with Adam and Eve, we must choose the light or love the darkness. John 3:19-20 says, "God's light came into the world, but people loved the darkness more than the light, for their actions were evil. All who do evil hate the light and refuse to go near it for fear their sins will be exposed." The Father's heart wants us back, and Jesus' life, death, and resurrection made it possible for us to become children of light.

This may be a far cry from the perception you have of God. Many believe that God is always angry and out to punish us, or that He's impatient and ready to strike us down when we sin. I recently prayed with a woman whose earthly father was physically and sexually abusive. Growing up, her view of God was distorted and tainted by her dad. We can never really feel God's love for us until we see God the Father for who He is. When we come to know the Father heart of God, we realize that He loves us so much that He wants us back, and we discover what He wants for us and has done for us. Here are just a few verses about what God has done, does, and will do for you when you come to Him:

- He has promised never to leave you nor forsake you (Deuteronomy 31:6, 8; Joshua 1:8; Psalm 94:14; Hebrews 13:5).

- He will supply all your needs (Psalms 23:1; 37:25; Philippians 4:19).

- You have access to Him at any time (Ephesians 2:18; Hebrews 4:16).

- He hears you when you pray (Psalm 66:19; Proverbs 15:29; John 9:31; 1 John 5:14).

- He gives you strength in overcoming evil desires and habits (Philippians 2:13; 4:13).

- He equips you with weapons for fighting the enemy in this world and in the heavenly places (2 Corinthians 10:4-5; Ephesians 6:10-20).

- He gives you good gifts (Matthew 7:9-11).

- If we claim Jesus as our Lord, our names are written down in the Lamb's Book of Life (Philippians 4:3; Revelation 13:8; 21:27).

- He has given you the Holy Spirit as your comforter and guide (John 14:16, 26; 16:13).

- He has given you an eternal inheritance in heaven (Ephesians 1:11; 1 Peter 1:3-4).

- If you are repentant, He does not hold one transgression against you (Psalms 32:1, 5; 103:12; Isaiah 38:17; 1 John 1:9; Romans 4:8).

- He delivers you from the kingdom of darkness into the kingdom of His Son (Colossians 1:13).

This is not an exhaustive list of what God the Father does for those who come to Him, but as you read through these Bible verses, please open your heart to the truth that God is a loving Father. In a world where unreal things happen every day, He offers real love to you. He is accessible at all times and approachable on your level. You don't have to have all the right words to say to Him. He cares for you and loves you like no one on Earth possibly could. He wants you to live a life that reflects His genuine love for you. He wants you back—period. You may be thinking that you were never on God's side to begin with, so how could He want you back? Because as you read a few pages earlier, even before He made the world, God loved you. He created you for relationship with Him, just as He created Adam and Eve for relationship with Him. Adam and Eve's sin separated them—just as it does the rest of humanity—from God. Perhaps in your wandering you have found yourself searching and longing for more, and God is ready with open arms. This world of madness may have pulled you away, but He wants you back.

THREE

Looking at the Creator of Love

I want my dad to love me, but he doesn't know how. Throughout my life, even today, I have felt like I am a disappointment to him." Melissa sat with me in one corner of the church and, with tears in her eyes, talked about her broken childhood. She is now close to 40 and has never felt the love of her earthly father. To say that she has a "father wound" would be an understatement. But what she does have and understands is the love of Father God.

"I don't know what my life would have been like if I didn't know God's love," she said.

Like Melissa, you may have a father who has never been able to offer love or who has never been involved in your life. If you're looking for God, you can know with certainty that He is near, that He will never abandon you, and that He will always love you. *Always*. To begin a search for God, it is important to start right here, with love. God is love and knows how to love because He has been loving from the very beginning, long before creation.

LOVE ORIGINATES WITH GOD

It was God's love that sent Jesus into the world to come and save us. In John 1:1-2, we read this about Jesus:

> In the beginning the Word already existed.
>   The Word was with God,
>   and the Word was God.
>   He existed in the beginning with God.

Verse 14 reveals who the Word is:

> The Word became human and made his home among us. He was full of unfailing love and faithfulness. And we have seen his glory, the glory of the Father's one and only Son.

The Word that became human and lived among us is the Father's one and only Son, Jesus. Notice that this verse says that when Jesus became human, He was "full of unfailing love and faithfulness." How could Jesus come to Earth and already be *full* of unfailing love and faithfulness? Because as John 1:1-2 says, He was God, and as 1 John 4:8 says, God is love. Matthew 1:23 says that Jesus was "God with us"—He was God in human flesh, and He came to share the Father's love with us. With you!

Unlike Melissa's father, a good father nurtures and loves his children. And love originates with the Father. First John 4:7-10 says,

> Dear friends, let us continue to love one another, for *love comes from God.* Anyone who loves is a child of God and knows God. But anyone who does not love does not know God, for God is love. God showed how much he loved us by sending his one and only Son into the world so that we might have eternal life through him. This is real love—not that we loved God, but that he loved us and sent his Son as a sacrifice to take away our sins (emphasis added).

These verses make it clear that love comes from God, and if we don't know God, then we won't have the capacity to love. But when we do know God, we will show love in our own lives because love pours from Him!

ELOHIM IS PLURAL

Genesis 1:1 says, "In the beginning God created the heavens and the earth." Most of the Old Testament was written in ancient Hebrew, and here, the Hebrew word for God is *Elohim*. In the very first verse of the Bible, God manifested Himself as Elohim, a *plural* form of the word. From the very beginning, God gave us an enormous clue about Himself and did not use a singular name but a *plural* one. There is an important reason for this!

You may have heard the term *Trinity* in connection with God. The Bible teaches that God the Father, God the Son, and God the Spirit are members of the Trinity (while the word *Trinity* is not found in the Bible, the truth of it is found throughout Scripture) and work together in our redemption. All three members of the Godhead are eternal and everlasting, omniscient (all-knowing), omnipotent (all-powerful), omnipresent (present in all places), and unchanging. While there are three persons in the Godhead, there is only one God. And there is no other god like God in this world. He says, "I am the Lord; there is no other God" (Isaiah 45:5).

THE TRIUNE GOD VERSUS SINGULAR GODS

As we just saw, the Bible says there is only one God. He reveals Himself to us as *Elohim*, which is a plural term in Hebrew. He is one, plural. That's why we can say the Trinity is not three gods, but three persons in one God: Father, Son, and Holy Spirit (we'll expand on this later), each sharing the same attributes yet fulfilling different functions in their roles in our lives. Tim Keller (1950–2023) said,

> The gospel writer John describes the Son as living from all eternity in the "bosom of the father" (John 1:18), an ancient metaphor for

love and intimacy. Later in John's Gospel, Jesus,
the Son, describes the Spirit as living to glorify
Him (John 16:14). In turn, the Son glorifies
the Father (17:4) and the Father the Son (17:5).
This has been going on for all eternity (17:5b).
What does the term "glorify" mean? To glorify something or someone is to praise, enjoy,
and delight in them…Each person of the Trinity loves, adores, defers to, and rejoices in the
others. The life of the Trinity is characterized
not by self-centeredness but by mutually self-
giving love.[1]

The Father has always been with the Son, and the Spirit
has always been with the Father and the Son. It was the
Son whom the Father sent to us to reveal His love for us,
and it is the Son who brings us close to the Father. "For
this is how God loved the world: He gave his one and only
Son, so that everyone who believes in him will not perish
but have eternal life" (John 3:16). And the Son said this
about the Spirit: "He will teach you everything and will
remind you of everything I have told you" (John 14:26).
In this, we see how all three members of the Trinity work
together in harmony for our good. And we see relationship
between them, which affirms how God is a relational God.

This brings us to an amazing truth about one of the
Holy Spirit's roles in the life of those who come to God.
Remember what we learned earlier about being adopted

into God's family? It is Christ who makes it possible to become part of that family, and it is the Spirit who confirms our adoption. Notice what Romans 8:14-16 says:

> All who are led by the Spirit of God are children of God. So you have not received a spirit that makes you fearful slaves. Instead, you received God's Spirit when he adopted you as his own children. Now we call him, "Abba, Father." For his Spirit joins with our spirit to affirm that we are God's children.

The Spirit confirms we are God's children, and this frees us from "a spirit that makes you fearful slaves"—that is, we no longer live in the fear caused by the devil and sin. God's Spirit does not make us slaves, but lets us know the freedom that comes with being children of God. The word "Abba" used here is Aramaic for *father*. "Abba" is a term of endearment, a term that speaks of tender love and care. Those who are children of God experience the Father's love in a special way. They do not receive a spirit that makes them fearful slaves, meaning that there *is* such a spirit that does exist in this world, but that spirit does not emanate from the Father of love. That spirit comes from the father of lies, the devil (John 8:44).

The God of the Bible is a relational God. As Tim Keller said, "Each person of the Trinity loves, adores, defers to, and rejoices in the others." God is so different from the gods of the man-made religions of this world. Many of these gods are singular in nature and not relational. A study of Apollo, Osiris, Diana, Venus, Marduk, Baal, or any other of the countless gods will prove they were not relational or compassionate or loving, but rather, were cold, distant, and loveless. They are the kinds of gods who would have slaves and subjects beneath them. None of these gods are accessible or fatherly in the way that the God of the Bible is, and none of them view their followers tenderly as children. Why would anyone want such gods to have any power over them?

Fouad Masri was born and raised in the war zone of Beirut, Lebanon, and is the founder and president of Crescent Project, which enables Christians to reach out to Muslim communities. "Islam demanded the worship of one god and no other," Fouad said in an email to me. "Allah in the Quran is transcendent (superior/supreme) from all humans. He is the almighty king and humans are the slaves. Allah is the judge on the judgment day, and each human must save themselves."

Unlike God the Father, who is relational with His children, Allah is singular. From Quran 112:1, 3 we read, "He is Allah—One and Indivisible. He has never had offspring, nor was he born." Allah "has never had offspring," meaning he does not have children. In a phone conversation with Masri, he said to me, "Quran 37:151-152 says, 'It is a lie if they say Allah has children.' This is another verse which proves that fatherhood is out for Allah. The idea that Allah is father and that we are children of God is not in the Quran. In the Bible, we have a Father who wants relationship with us. Who wants fellowship with us. In the Quran, god is the master of humankind; you are the slave."

In Quran 4:171, it is made abundantly clear that Allah is alone and only one god when it says, "The Messiah, Jesus, son of Mary, was no more than a messenger of Allah and the fulfillment of His Word through Mary and a spirit created by a command from Him. So believe in Allah and His messengers, and do not say, 'Trinity.' Stop!—for your own good. Allah is only One God. Glory be to Him! He is far above having a son!"

Allah is on his own, he is "far above having a son." There is no one with him to love. How does he love, how does he connect, how does Allah relate to anyone without having anyone with him to love? He doesn't.

GOD THE FATHER OR THE BEST DECEIVER

"None of Allah's creatures are like Him"[2] (Quran 112:4). There are some people who believe that Allah and God are the same, but Allah is not the same as the Father God found in the Bible, who said, "Let us make human beings in our image, to be like us" (Genesis 1:26). Notice the pronouns here: Let *us* make human beings in *our* image. The

Father was not alone in creating us; Jesus and the Holy Spirit were with Him. And unlike Allah's creatures, who are not like him, we were created to be like God our Father.

As our Father, we are told, among many things, that God is good and faithful and full of mercy. He cares and provides for us. He hears us and answers us when we pray. He delivers and rescues us. He welcomes us with open arms and forgives us. He wants the best for us, will only speak truth to us, and will never lie to nor deceive us (Psalms 100:5; 145:9; Daniel 6:27; Matthew 6:25-34; 7:7-11; Hebrews 12:3-11; Luke 15:11-32; John 10:10; 17:17; 1 Samuel 15:29).

Unlike God the Father, in the Quran we read that Allah is the "best deceiver." Allah is said to be the "best deceiver" in the following verses: 3:54; 7:99; 8:30; 10:21; and 13:42.[3] The root word in all these verses is *makr,* which means "deception" and describes someone as sly and dishonest. It was Allah's deception that made Mohammed's (the founder of Islam) best friend and father-in-law, Abu Bakr (who was one of ten men guaranteed entry into paradise), despair of his salvation. When reassured of his position in Allah, Bakr once stated, "By Allah! I would not rest assured and feel safe from the deception of Allah, even if I had one foot in paradise."[4]

In one particular hadith (stories and reports of what

Mohammed said and did, which are revered by Muslims as a major source of religious law and moral guidance),[5] Mohammed stood at the side of a dead man and said, "As to him, by Allah, death has overtaken him, and I hope the best for him. By Allah, *though I am the Apostle of Allah, yet I do not know what Allah will do to me*"[6] (emphasis added). Mohammed's best friend and Mohammed himself could not trust Allah with their salvation because Allah is not all-loving and merciful.

Michael Reeves, author of *Delighting in the Trinity*, says, "Thus the only God inherently inclined to show mercy is the Father who has eternally loved his Son by the Spirit. Only with this God do such winning qualities as love and mercy rank highly."[7]

1 X 1 X 1 = 1

Many faiths, Islam included, look at Christianity and say that 1 God + 1 God + 1 God = 3 Gods, but that is not a correct representation of the Trinity. We may have a hard time wrapping our mind around the concept of the Trinity, but as I wrote earlier, the Trinity is not three gods, but three persons in one God, each acting with unique roles yet one in essence. Often, when Fouad Masri is talking with Muslims, he will reason with them that instead of using addition when thinking about the Trinity (1 + 1 + 1 = 3), to instead use multiplication. "Think about it this way: 1 × 1 × 1 equals 1. The triune God isn't a matter of addition, but multiplication—three goes into one and makes a whole. We're human; we are limited. God's character is above our reason…The logic of the Trinity is far above our logic. It is God's domain."[8] The Trinity is a mystery and beyond our complete understanding, but Christians believe the teaching about the Trinity by faith because God has made the Trinity known to us throughout the Bible, and God cannot lie (Numbers 23:19; Titus 1:2; Hebrews 6:18).

ABOVE ALL REASON

In 1 Corinthians 8:4-7, we read,

> "There is no God but one." For even if there are so-called gods, whether in heaven or on earth (as indeed there are many "gods" and many "lords"), yet for us there is but one God, the Father, from whom all things came and for whom we live; and there is but one Lord, Jesus Christ, through whom all things came and through whom we live. But not everyone possesses this knowledge (NIV).

There is one God, one Lord, "but not everyone possesses this knowledge." Jesus said, "The Father and I are one" (John 10:30). They are one—not many. Romans 10:13 says, "Everyone who calls on the name of the LORD will be saved." The Bible says to call on *one* name, not many, and that is the name of the Lord alone. Acts 4:12 tells us, "There is salvation in no one else! God has given no other name under heaven by which we must be saved." Salvation is not found anywhere else except in the name of Jesus. Jesus said, "I am the way, the truth, and the life. No one can come to the Father except through me" (John 14:6). One way. Not many. Only the cross of Jesus leads us to the Father.

You may be struggling with "salvation in no one else" because you were raised in a different religion or you've heard there are many ways to God. Or maybe you have family or friends who believe in many gods. God, as the good Father, wants you to come to Him with your questions and doubts.

In Acts 17, we read that when the apostle Paul was in Athens, his spirit was provoked because he saw that the city was given over to idols. He noticed many altars and religious objects of worship. One altar was inscribed, "To an Unknown God," which was the perfect setup for Paul to tell the people about the one true God (verses 16, 22-34). Of Jesus' birth we read, "The virgin will conceive a child! She will give birth to a son, and they will call him Immanuel, which means 'God is with us'" (Matthew 1:23—I cover Jesus' birth, the names and places associated with it, and the reason He came in the book *Looking for Christmas*). Jesus said that His Father "offers you the true bread from heaven. The true bread of God is the one who comes down from heaven and gives life to the world" (John 6:32-33). Only one God came from heaven to give us life. Not many gods.

More than a decade ago, my husband and I were part of a humanitarian trip to visit orphanages in India. We would often see little shrines set up along the roadway, and at one point I said to our interpreter, "I heard somewhere that India has something like 30,000 gods that are worshipped here. Is that true?"

She chuckled and said, "Oh, no! There are 330 million gods, meaning that there are an infinite number of them!"

I can't begin to wrap my mind around the chaos and confusion of attempting to serve or understand 330 million gods, or even a small fraction of that. A friend of mine recalled that a Hindu coworker said, "Christians don't seem to like that we have multiple gods, but they have three gods that they claim to serve: God, Jesus, and Mary." This common misconception has endured for centuries among people of other faiths. Muslims also view Mary, the mother of Jesus, as part of the Trinity, and they view the Trinity as a form of blasphemy because others (Jesus and Mary, in this case) are being treated as equal with God.

Christianity celebrates the complex oneness of the

triune God. At the baptism of Jesus in Luke 3:21-22, we see each person of the Trinity represented: God the Father, God the Holy Spirit, and Jesus, God the Son. When speaking to His disciples, Jesus stated the reality of the Trinity in Matthew 28:19, "Go and make disciples of all the nations, baptizing them in the name of the Father and the Son and the Holy Spirit."

Again, it is impossible for us to fully understand the complex nature and mystery of God. Are you prepared to not completely understand His nature? To realize and embrace that His nature is above all reason? Evelyn Underhill said, "If God were small enough to be understood, He would not be big enough to be worshipped."[9] The fact that the avowed atheist C.S. Lewis couldn't understand the meaning of the crucifixion, the resurrection, or of redemption is what held him back from belief in God until he was in his thirties. At one point, he wondered aloud to his friend J.R.R. Tolkien if he was demanding too much of the mystery.[10] The following week, Lewis rode in the sidecar of his brother's motorcycle as they headed toward Whipsnade Zoo in England. The trip was a little over 30 miles long, but to Lewis, the trip spanned 2,000 years. He could not explain what took place during that ride; it was above his reasoning. All he knew was that when he climbed out of that sidecar, he embraced the mystery and believed in Jesus.

The Trinity is a mystery that we will never fully comprehend. Like C.S. Lewis, are you open to embracing the mystery and believing? For you, believing in God may be only one sidecar ride, one dip in the ocean, one hike up a hillside, one workout at the gym, one celebration with family, one boat trip on a lake, or one coffee with a friend away.

FOUR

Looking at the God Who Sees You

my is a beautiful woman in her late forties. She is a busy wife and mother of four, and loaded with creativity and skills. One day as I was praying, God brought her to mind, and I began to pray for her. I knew some things about Amy but little about her childhood. In my mind's eye, I saw her as a little girl around eight to ten years old, lying in her bed at night. She heard something and got up and went into her little brother's room and cared for him, mothering and comforting him. She left his room and went into another sibling's room, where she did the same, caring for and comforting that sibling. She then went back to her own room and lay back down. I could sense that she felt very lonely, abandoned, and unseen, and she thought, *Who is mothering me? Who is fathering me?* And God instantly whispered to her spirit, "I am, Amy. I am...and I'm still doing it today."

Immediately, I wondered if what I saw in my mind was from God or just stray thoughts. Part of me felt that I should share this with Amy, but the other part thought, *No way! That could've been my own thoughts.* So, I didn't tell her. I would often see her at church and think about what had happened, but I didn't mention it to her. I held on to that image of her as a child for nearly a year and a half. Every now and then, something inside of me would want to call her and tell her about it, but I didn't. If that image of her was truly from God, then I wanted to be sure of that before I said anything.

One day, as I was driving to pick up my son at school, a sense of urgency came over me, as if God was saying, "Call Amy now and tell her." I kept driving, and again, I sensed, "Call Amy now!"

When I came to the next stoplight, I dialed Amy's number, and because of her busy schedule, I assumed she wouldn't answer. But she did. She was in her car and had time to chat. I told her about praying for her more than a year and a half earlier, and how God had given me an image of her as a little girl. I explained that I had held on to this image for so long because I just wasn't sure if it was from God or from my own thoughts. I relayed to her exactly what I had seen, including her thought, *Who is mothering me? Who is fathering me?* And I shared about God's reply, "I am, Amy. I am…and I'm still doing it today."

Amy was quiet on the other end, and I hoped that I hadn't wasted her time when suddenly she whispered, "I can't see because I'm crying so much."

"Does that mean something to you?" I asked.

"Yes. I can't even…I'm crying so much."

I apologized for not sharing this with her earlier and said I was embarrassed it had taken me a year and a half to share this with her.

"This came at the right time," she said.

Amy and her brothers grew up in a home where they were often left alone. Addiction and other negative choices lured Amy's parents away, leaving her with the overwhelming sense that she had to care for her brothers. She desperately wanted her parents to love her and her siblings, to meet her deepest needs and provide a safe home filled with happiness and laughter, but they didn't do that. Although she was only a child at the time and one brother was older by 13 months, it was Amy who felt the weight and responsibility of caring for her siblings. She often felt unseen, unloved, and forgotten, but God says He will not forget Amy or any of us. "Can a mother forget the baby at her breast and have no compassion on the child she has borne? Though she may forget, I will not forget you!" (Isaiah 49:15 NIV).

We carry high hopes when we put our trust in someone; but we often fail to realize that humans have limitations, and when someone doesn't measure up to our expectations, we face deep disappointments. If we are hurt multiple times in relationships, we often push people away entirely. You may have been hurt so many times that you have pushed God away, blaming Him for the hurt that others have caused you. You may think that God doesn't care for or see you in your pain.

GOD TAKES NOTICE OF YOU

In Genesis 16, Hagar is pregnant with Abraham's baby, and Abraham's wife, Sarai, begins to mistreat her. Sarai turns up the heat so badly against Hagar that Hagar runs away into the wilderness. She doesn't have a plan or a map of the wilderness; she just runs. Verse 7 says that "the angel of the Lord" found her (notice that it doesn't say "an angel," but rather, "the Angel of the Lord" [NKJV], with the word *angel* capitalized. This is no ordinary angel, but what many scholars believe is the Son of God in a special appearance before He came to Earth in human flesh).

If He found her, that means He had been looking for her. Hagar was important to God. And the baby whom she carried inside of her was important to God. The angel of the Lord told Hagar to return to Sarai, and said she would have a son. He then blessed her with these words in verse 11: "You are to name him Ishmael (which means 'God hears'), for the Lord has heard your cry of distress."

And Hagar responded, "You are the God who sees me" (verse 13).

God heard and saw a pregnant woman running away through the wilderness, and He blessed her right where she was. Similarly, God heard and saw Amy when she was a little girl caring for her brothers just as He continues to hear and see her today.

For 400 years, the Hebrew people had been enslaved in Egypt. It seemed as if God had forgotten His children, but He heard their groanings and cries (Exodus 2:23-24). Verse 25 says, "God saw the sons of Israel, and God took notice of them" (NASB).

"God took notice of them." God, the Creator of the entire universe, is all-powerful and all-knowing, yet He took notice of a pregnant woman running through the wilderness, and of a little girl in her bed alone at night worrying about her brothers. He also takes notice of you and me, in whatever condition we find ourselves in. As the Israelites found themselves in distress, Isaiah 63:9 says of God, "In all their suffering he also suffered." He is not a God who is uncaring and unfeeling. He feels our suffering. His desire is that you would not keep Him at a distance, for He loves you. He hears you and sees you and wants a relationship with you.

YOU WERE CREATED FOR RELATIONSHIP

Human relationships can disappoint, and we were not created to be alone. We were created for relationship with one another and with God (Genesis 2:18; Ecclesiastes 4:9-12; Acts 2:42; Hebrews 10:24-25). We can trust God with our emotions, feelings, and desires. We can cast all our needs on Him because He is a good, loving, powerful, reliable, and consistent Father. You can look to Him for security instead of to other people. God will not fail you.

Once we realize and receive the love that He has for us, how we look at our human relationships will change. We will look to God to meet our deepest needs and not our spouse, parent, boyfriend, girlfriend, child, or any other relationship. The Bible says that God loves us with an everlasting love (Jeremiah 31:3). He quiets us with His love, and as I mentioned in the story about Nicole from chapter 1, He rejoices over us with singing (Zephaniah 3:17). Is there anyone else in your life who quiets your soul by singing over you? He loves you so much that He sent His dearly beloved Son to Earth to save and redeem you so that you could live in eternity with Him forever.

> God showed how much he loved us by sending his one and only Son into the world so that we might have eternal life through him. This is real love—not that we loved God, but that he

loved us and sent his Son as a sacrifice to take
away our sins (1 John 4:9-10).

God loved you first! You were created to be loved. You
were created to be in relationship and not alone.

We tend to spend more time with someone once we get
to know them better. When we begin to date someone, we
usually don't go back for a second date if we aren't com-
fortable with that person's personality. Much of our stress
and displeasure in the workplace is due to the personalities
of those around us. The more we are around someone, the
more we get to know them for good or bad.

One-quarter of former atheists (24 percent) reported
that care and concern from Christians attracted them
toward God after a personal crisis.[1] It was relationships
with believers that changed the hearts of these former
atheists toward God. It was Christians showing care and
concern and reaching out to them in personal ways that
transformed their lives. Atheists got to know the personality of God through Christ followers. How did those
believers get to know the personality of God? By being in
a relationship with Him and reading His Word. The more
time we spend with God, the more we get to know His
personality, and the more He is able to shine through us.

THE NAMES OF GOD REVEAL HIS HEART

So much of who God is can be found in His names.

There are many names for God in the Bible. This is not an exhaustive list by any means, but I asked my friends on Facebook for the names that meant the most to them. These were the most popular responses.

> Abba, which means "father" (Romans 8:15)
>
> Our Hope (Jeremiah 29:11; Romans 15:13; 1 Peter 1:3)
>
> El Roi, the God who sees me (Genesis 16:13)
>
> Wonderful Counselor (Isaiah 9:6)
>
> Our Peace (Judges 6:24; Isaiah 9:6)
>
> Our Guide (Psalm 48:14)
>
> Our Deliverer (2 Samuel 22:2; Psalm 18:2)
>
> Our Keeper (Psalm 121:5)
>
> The Good Shepherd (John 10:11)
>
> Our Healer (Exodus 15:26; Psalm 147:3; Matthew 9:12)
>
> Our Helper (Psalm 54:4; Isaiah 41:10; Hebrews 13:6)
>
> Our Strength (Psalm 27:1; Philippians 4:13)
>
> Friend of Sinners (Matthew 11:19)
>
> Our Provider (Genesis 22:14; Psalm 147:8; Matthew 6:26; Philippians 4:19)

Our Savior (Isaiah 43:11; Hosea 13:4; Psalms 18:2; 118:14; Luke 2:11; Acts 13:23; Titus 2:13)

Our Teacher (Exodus 4:15; Psalms 25:12; 32:8; Isaiah 2:3; John 13:13)

Our Stability (Numbers 23:19; Hebrews 13:8; James 1:17)

Think of how many of the various gods from the world's religions it would take to equal our God Most High (Psalm 57:2)! When we look at His names, we can see what His heart is toward us. Our God loves us so much that He provides everything that we need through Him! God's love is not based on what we do or how we perform or whether we have fulfilled a list of expectations from Him. His love is not earned, and it can't be taken away. This is what separates Christianity from other religions. If God's love for His own isn't unconditional, then His Word is filled with lies.

LOVE SOMEONE TO DEATH

About a year ago, a friend took a few days to post online about God's love. The various posts said things like, "God is love." True. "God loves everyone." True. "You don't have to do anything more. His love is enough. Just let Him love you." I read the many comments in response to the posts, and they were all applauding the brilliance of these statements. Around day four of the posts, I agreed with everything that my friend had been saying about God's love. But I added that we have to choose to respond to that love or not. I cited John 1:12, which says, "As many as *received* Him, to them He gave the right to become children of God, to those who *believe* in His name" (NASB, emphasis added).

I had no idea the pushback that would create! People on my friend's page couldn't believe that I said a person has to receive God's love and become His child by believing in Jesus' name. My friend was so angry at my comments that a blog was then written, quoting me but without reference to John 1:12 about the need to receive and believe in Jesus.

Like my friend, we can say "God loves you" until someone's dying breath, but that person can still have hate in their heart toward God and reject Him. We can love someone straight into an eternity without God because we never share the simple truth that a person has to take some action in response to God's love. We have to receive and believe in Jesus as Lord and Savior. Otherwise, people end up depending on self-salvation and being their own saviors and lords.

British journalist Malcolm Muggeridge (1903–1990) interviewed Joseph Stalin's daughter Svetlana on a BBC documentary about her father. She recalled that while her father was on his deathbed, he raised himself up with what strength he had and shook his fists toward the heavens.[2] Early in his life, Stalin had been a seminary student. Surely, he had heard that God loved him, but he did not receive that love or believe in the name of Jesus, and one of his final actions on earth was to express defiance toward God. We can say, "God loves you! God loves you! God loves you!" and someone can still shake their fists at God on their deathbed. Action is required by a person to receive His love and believe in His name. Either we belong to Him, or we don't.

The very purpose of the Bible is to reveal God's love for us. Jesus came from the Father to show His love for us and invite us into the kingdom of light. He leads us with "cords of kindness, with the bands of love" (Hosea 11:4 esv). We simply receive and believe!

FIVE

Looking at Our Helper

When God looks at mankind, He sees His creation in two distinct groups of people: His children who have the Spirit living inside of them (those who have received and believed), and unbelievers who do not have the Spirit (those who may have heard about God's love but so far, have rejected it). The Holy Spirit makes Christ a reality to each believer (Ephesians 3:16-17) and is, in fact, called the Spirit of Christ. Romans 8:9 says, "You are controlled by the Spirit if you have the Spirit of God living in you. (And remember that those who do not have the Spirit of Christ living in them do not belong to him at all.)" If you don't have the Spirit of Christ living in you, then you don't belong to Him. We simply can't argue with that. We either have the Spirit of God and belong to Him or we don't.

The spirit is that which is eternal in a person. The New Testament Greek word for spirit, *pneuma,* translates roughly to "breath"; for a Christian, it is the living essence that connects the body, heart, and mind, and will return to God when he or she dies.[1] When Jesus was dying on the cross, He shouted, "'Father, I entrust my spirit into your hands!' And with those words he breathed his last." The word *heart* is similar, but it usually describes the soul—the will, mind, and emotions.

For Christians, if it were not for the Holy Spirit, we would be groping our way through life without courage or faith. Those who ended up becoming part of the early church lacked boldness and power (in fact, they fled and hid when Jesus was arrested in the garden) *until* the promised Holy Spirit was poured out on them in Acts chapter 2. Jesus had told them, "You will receive power when the Holy Spirit has come upon you. And you will be my witnesses, telling people about me everywhere" (Acts 1:8). The early church believed the word of Jesus when He told them to wait in Jerusalem for the Holy Spirit. They received the Spirit with the expectation that He would help them do great things, and that they would walk in His power.

When the Holy Spirit took up residence in the lives of those believers, power came to them that enabled them to tell people everywhere about the love of Jesus. Jesus also told them that they would be persecuted and brought before kings and councils, but said, "When you are arrested and stand trial, don't worry in advance about what to say. Just say what God tells you at that time, for it is not you who will be speaking, but the Holy Spirit" (Mark 13:11).

The early believers were active and powerful *because* of the Holy Spirit working in each of their lives. He truly was their Helper. The early church would have floundered and died without this power. Those early believers learned how to walk in the Spirit and how to lean on Him for guidance, and as a result, they turned the world upside down as they shared the love of God.

A.W. Tozer once said, "If the Holy Spirit was withdrawn from the church today, 95 percent of what we do would go on and no one would know the difference. If the Holy Spirit had been withdrawn from the New Testament church, 95 percent of what they did would stop, and everybody would know the difference."[2]

LIKE A DOVE

Ephesians 4:30 tells us not to grieve the Holy Spirit of God. In this verse, the definition of the Greek word translated "grieve" means "to be sad, cause grief, be in heaviness, make sorry."[3] When we ignore the Holy Spirit's promptings and nudgings, we can literally make Him sad and cause Him grief and heaviness. Oswald Chambers said, "He does not come with a voice of thunder, but with a voice so gentle that it is easy to ignore it."[4] Those who are

Christians need to decide whose voice they will listen to, and in a chaotic, unreal world, it is far too easy to ignore the gentle voice of the Holy Spirit.

It's interesting to note that when John the Baptist baptized Jesus, he said, "I saw the Spirit descending from heaven like a dove, and He remained upon Him. I did not know Him, but He who sent me to baptize with water said to me, 'Upon whom you see the Spirit descending, and remaining on Him, this is He who baptizes with the Holy Spirit'" (John 1:32-33 NKJV).

Twice, John said the Spirit descended and remained on Jesus, which tells us this fact is important. Each year, two doves build a nest outside our home. The slightest noise drives them away. Doves and pigeons are functionally the same, but they are nothing alike. You can walk through the middle of pigeons and they will barely move, but a dove will quickly take flight. They are far more sensitive than pigeons. When a Christian sins and grieves the Holy Spirit, his or her conscience can become dead through the practice of that sin (1 Timothy 4:2), and that hinders the Spirit's engagement with that person. A true believer in Christ will always have the Holy Spirit within them, but the Spirit's work in that person's life will not be fully known if they are living in a way that grieves the Spirit. God is love (1 John 4:8), but He is also holy, holy, holy (Isaiah 6:3; Revelation 4:8), and He can't tolerate sin.

THE GREAT INVADER

When we look at the ways the third person of the Trinity operates in a Christian's life, we understand how He loves and cares for them. Here is a short list of how the Holy Spirit operates:

- ⚘ The Holy Spirit sent Jesus for our healing, freedom, restoration, and salvation (Luke 4:18-19).

- ⚘ The Holy Spirit testifies with a Christian's spirit that they are children of God (Romans 8:15-16).

- ⚘ The Holy Spirit teaches Christ's followers all things (Luke 12:12; John 14:26).

- ⚘ For Christians, the Holy Spirit is a comforter and advocate (John 14:26). *Merriam-Webster* defines *comforter* as "Holy Spirit. One that gives comfort."[5] The dictionary literally recognizes the Holy Spirit as a comforter! He is a believer's comforter and advocate, meaning that He pleads their cause before God.

- ⚘ The Holy Spirit invites people into the kingdom of God (Revelation 22:17).

- ⚘ The Spirit will cause believers to walk in the ways of God (Ezekiel 36:27).

- ⚘ The Holy Spirit points people to Jesus (John 15:26).

I met a woman years ago who grew up in India surrounded by the worship of idols and false gods, but deep inside, she longed for something more. She said that when she was 17 she prayed, "If there is one true God, please show me the way to You." And guess what? In a country with 330 million gods, the Holy Spirit led her to Jesus, and her life was radically changed!

Romans 8:11 says, "Just as God raised Christ Jesus from the dead, he will give life to your mortal bodies by this same Spirit living within You." When you claim Jesus as Lord, the Holy Spirit takes up residence inside of you and gives life to your mortal body. He will invigorate you to new life, like seeds that have been germinating in the soil and begin to spring up and grow. In *My Utmost for His Highest,* Oswald Chambers (1874–1917) said, "The Holy Spirit cannot be located as a Guest in the house, He invades everything."[6] In other words, He is the Great Invader!

WALKING IN THE SPIRIT

I know a woman who claims to be a follower of Jesus, but she treats her widowed mother horribly. She talks to her dog in a kinder tone than she does to her mom. She will tell her mom she hates her, then hang the phone up on her. Does she sound like anyone you would want to be around?

When I look at the fruit of the Spirit—love, joy, peace,

patience, kindness, goodness, faithfulness, gentleness, and self-control—I don't see it in this "Christian" woman. She is self-centered and bitter, and it is impossible to see any trace of the Spirit within her. As I have stated previously, the members of the Trinity have loved each other for all eternity. Their love has always been other-directed. We were made for this other-directed kind of love. Self-centeredness destroys this love that God has created for Christians to share.

On a Christian's very best day, and in their greatest strength, they can never act like Jesus. That's why Jesus promised to send a Helper, the Holy Spirit. When we accept the free gift of salvation offered through Jesus, then the Holy Spirit comes to live inside of us (1 Corinthians 3:16; 6:19). But life throws us curveballs, and even after becoming a believer, we often look to ourselves and other things for help instead of to the Helper. A friend told me about an argument she had with her husband, and said, "It's nothing that three or four drinks can't handle." We have all been there; maybe we haven't turned to drinking, but we may have turned to something or someone else to ease the pain of an argument or a difficult situation.

When left to our own devices, we would be totally given over to self-gratification. In Galatians 5, Paul said that it is for freedom that Christ sets people free, stating, "Stand fast therefore in the liberty by which Christ has made us free, and do not be entangled again with a yoke of bondage," and "do not use liberty as an opportunity for the flesh" (Galatians 5:1, 13 NKJV).

Paul was saying that Jesus came so that the Galatians would have abundant life, but he did not want them to use that beautiful, life-giving freedom to feed the flesh (to indulge in self-gratification, self-absorption, self-centeredness). He went on to list the acts of the flesh in Galatians 5:19-22: "When you follow the desires of your sinful nature, the results are very clear: sexual immorality, impurity, lustful pleasures, idolatry, sorcery, hostility, quarreling, jealousy, outbursts of anger, selfish ambition, dissension, division, envy, drunkenness, wild parties, and other sins like these. Let me tell you again, as I have before, that anyone living that sort of life will not inherit the Kingdom of God." Like the woman I mentioned earlier who is cruel to her mom, we can never live a free and abundant life when we are in bondage to any of the behaviors on that list. As you read God's Word, He will reveal to you the differences between the Spirit and the flesh, and you will learn how to listen for His voice. This is part of the journey with God. Philippians 1:6 encourages believers, saying, "I am certain that God, who began the good work within you, will continue his work until it is finally finished on the day when Christ Jesus returns." When God begins a good work in you, He will finish it!

Paul said to believers in Galatians 5:25, "Since we are living by the Spirit, let us follow the Spirit's leading in every part of our lives." To follow the Spirit's leading is not a Sunday-only event; it is a continual way of life. When people live in the Spirit, they have His help in turning from the sins they have participated in.

When you are a Christian, with the Holy Spirit's help, you are sensitive to the Spirit's conviction of your sins, and you turn back to God. Paul said in Philippians 2:13, "God is working in you, giving you the desire and the power to do what pleases him." Most of the problems Christians face would be solved if they were more aware of the Holy Spirit in their lives. He is not a bully; He loves those who are in Christ, and He will never shame them as He reminds them of the toll that sin is taking on their life. When the Holy Spirit is allowed to do His work, the result is a life of freedom, peace, joy, and power!

SIX

Looking at God's Word

George Muller (1805–1898) relied solely on his faith in God to help him raise up homes to shelter and feed orphans in England. It is said that these homes cared for more than 10,000 orphans during his lifetime. Amazingly, Muller never asked for any donations. He would simply read God's Word and pray, relying on God and His Word to meet the needs. He said, "God is the author of the Bible, and only the truth it contains will lead people to true happiness." Muller relied on the truth of God's Word to lead him and the orphans he cared for to true happiness. God's Word still does that today.

IT IS A LIVING WORD

You may be on a path of discovery about God, but maybe you take issue with His Word, the Bible. Perhaps I have already shared verses that you find offensive or hard to believe. So this may be a good time to examine the validity of the Bible before we go any further. Maybe you struggle with the idea that this ancient text could possibly be true. Or maybe someone in your life has used the Bible as a weapon against you. You might question what makes it believable. After all, there are people today who teach that if you say something with enough feeling and power, that will somehow make it true. Today, people have their own personal truth, which makes God's truth irrelevant or meaningless. What makes the Bible's truths more valid than other ancient or modern texts? You might think it is so ancient that it couldn't possibly be relevant today.

However, as A.W. Tozer said,

> God is forever seeking to speak Himself out to His creation. The whole Bible supports the idea. God is speaking. Not God spoke, but God is speaking...God did not write a book and send it by messenger to be read at a distance by unaided minds. He spoke a book and lives in His spoken words, constantly speaking His words, and causing the power of them to persist across the years...The tragedy is that our eternal welfare depends upon our hearing, and we have trained our ears not to hear...I think a new world will arise out of the religious mists when we approach our Bible with the idea that it is not only a book which was once spoken, but a book which is now speaking. If you would follow on to know the Lord,

come at once to the open Bible, expecting it
to speak to you. Do not come with the notion
that it is a thing which you may push around
at your convenience. It is more than a thing;
it is a voice, a word, the very word of the living God.[1]

GOD EXALTS HIS WORD ABOVE HIS NAME

Many people say that the Bible simply *contains* God's
Word, which can easily give the impression that not all of
it is binding. This can lead people to picking and choos-
ing what parts they want to believe or not believe, which
questions the authority and reliability of God's Word. But
the Bible doesn't simply contain God's Word; it *is* God's
Word. Jesus said to the Father in John 17:17, "Your word
is truth" (NIV). God's Word is so important to Him that
Psalm 138:2 says, "You have magnified Your word above all
Your name" (NKJV). R.T. Kendall, former pastor at West-
minster Chapel in London, England, researched this verse
to make sure that it means what it says, and one of the
men he contacted was Rabbi Sir David Rosen, an Ortho-
dox Jew in Jerusalem. Kendall says, "Here is what he wrote
to me: The translation should be, 'You have exalted your
word (or Your speech) above Your Name,' i.e., the Divine
Word is more important to Him than His Name."[2]

"People do not live by bread alone; rather, we live by

every word that comes from the mouth of the LORD" (Deuteronomy 8:3). Those who belong to God live by every word that comes from the mouth of God! The verse doesn't say the word that "came," but rather "comes," which is in the present and active tense. The present and active Word comes from the mouth of God and sustains His people. "From His mouth comes knowledge and understanding" (Proverbs 2:6). Our lives are meant to depend on God's Word!

First Thessalonians 2:13 says, "When you received the word of God, which you heard from us, you accepted it not as a human word, but as it actually is, the word of God, which is indeed at work in you who believe" (NIV). The Word of God is at work in those who believe because it is living and active. God's Word isn't dead. It isn't some dull, ancient text sitting on a bookshelf. It is alive and powerful for living life today (Hebrews 4:12).

Numbers 23:19 tells us that "God is not a man, so he does not lie," and Proverbs 30:5 says, "Every word of God proves true." Second Timothy 3:16 says, "All Scripture is breathed out by God and profitable for teaching, for reproof, for correction, and for training in righteousness" (ESV).

NO OTHER RELIGIOUS TEXT CAN MAKE THESE CLAIMS

No other religious text on Earth can make those claims

because all of them were written by men from their own minds and thoughts. Yes, every book in the Bible was written by men and eyewitnesses of the events that happened. But their writings were God-breathed, rather than from human minds (2 Timothy 3:16; 2 Peter 1:20-21). They were human and flawed, of course, but when these men wrote the books of the Bible, as R.T. Kendall states,

> God overruled, and we can embrace Paul's words wholeheartedly. So too with Matthew, Mark, Luke, and John, as well as the Old Testament and all of the rest of the New Testament writers. You may safely read all of Scripture, knowing that the same faithful God who sent His Son into the world to die on a cross, made sure His Son's words were recorded without error and the apostles chosen to write what we call the New Testament gave us infallible teaching. God would not send His Son to us and then allow what He came to do to be forgotten. That is why we have the Bible.[3]

The Bible even makes it clear that there are things within it that are hard to understand, but the writers wrote with wisdom that was given to them by God. However, there are many people who twist the words of the Bible to mean something other than what they say. Look at what 2 Peter 3:15-16 says about Paul's writings: "Some of his comments are hard to understand, and those who are ignorant and unstable have twisted his letters to mean something quite different, just as they do with other parts of Scripture. And this will result in their destruction." Yes, some of God's words are hard to understand, but it doesn't end well when we twist His words to give them a different meaning. Peter warns us that this results in our destruction.

Nothing in the Bible ever came out of man's flesh, but through God. In 2 Peter 1:20-21, we read, "Above all, you must realize that no prophecy in Scripture ever came from the prophet's own understanding, or from human initiative. No, those prophets were moved by the Holy Spirit, and they spoke from God." The Spirit of God was at work and moving as He guided each of the 40 authors in recording what God was saying. In the Bible, we see phrases like, "God spoke to Abraham," or "Thus says the LORD," or "The LORD said to Isaiah." The words are God-breathed and of divine origin, not human.

The apostle Paul said, "Therefore, we never stop thanking God that when you received his message from us, you didn't think of our words as mere human ideas. You accepted what we said as the very word of God—which, of course, it is. And this word continues to work in you who believe" (1 Thessalonians 2:13). Like the believers in ancient Thessalonica, you will need to decide whether the

Bible is mere human ideas, or if you will accept it as the very word of God. When you come to the point of belief that it is the very word of God, the Bible will do its work in your life. As you read, it will bring you closer to God as you learn His truth. When you read the Bible, your faith will increase, and you will grow in God's love and grace. The good news of the gospel will give you hope, peace, and joy. It will become life-giving and real to you amid the unreal things that happen in this world.

WHAT MAKES THE BIBLE TRUTH?

The Bible is filled with actual, reliable historical facts. In a Gallup poll, 29 percent of Americans said they believe the Bible is a collection of "fables, legends, history and moral precepts recorded by man." A new low of 20 percent believe that it is the literal word of God.[4]

However, even non-Christian sources and archaeology verify the many historical facts that appear in both the Old and New Testaments. Each historical account describes real people facing real situations; they were as human as you or me.

There are 66 books in the Bible: 39 in the Old Testament and 27 in the New. Many were written by actual eyewitnesses of the events they documented. All of these books were written over a period of 1,500 years by 40 authors, many of whom didn't know each other. What is amazing is that they all told *one* story over those 1,500 years—God's redeeming love story!

If you have ever played the game of telephone, you know that the statement given to the first person in the game changes significantly by the time it reaches the last person. The only way these 40 authors could tell one story over 1,500 years is because the messages they wrote all came from God. The New Testament presents the Old Testament as authentic, quoting hundreds of passages and confirming the supernatural events that took place in the Old Testament.

Ultimately, there is no other book like the Bible in the entire world! But people say, "Times change. We live in an entirely different culture than that of the Bible. It's so ancient! How can we trust what we read in it today?"

AMAZING EVIDENCE

Think through some of these facts: There are 5,856 Greek New Testament manuscripts in existence today that total more than 2.6 million pages. Of non-Greek manuscripts (Armenian, Latin, etc.), there are more than 18,130, bringing the total Bible manuscripts in existence today to 28,986.[5] Compare those numbers to Plato's *Tetralogies*, written in AD 895 and having just over 200 manuscripts in existence. Or the earliest manuscripts of plays by Sophocles from the third century, with about 200 manuscripts.[6] Caesar's *Gallic Wars*, written in the first century, has 10 ancient manuscripts in existence.

Some people say that the nearly 6,000 Greek New Testament manuscripts that exist today could have easily been altered. But what about the existing manuscripts of Plato, Caesar, or Sophocles? Nobody is debating whether their words have been changed, and there are far fewer manuscripts available of their writings.

You cannot find any literature from antiquity with more evidence of authenticity than the Bible with its 28,986 New Testament manuscripts in existence! Some critics say that these manuscripts contain differences in the texts, but the variants are minor, including spelling variations. Those small differences don't change the message.

Some may say, "Well, those manuscripts could have easily been changed." Let's take a closer look at the evidence. If anyone would have wanted to change the New Testament manuscripts, they would have had to go to superhuman measures.

- First, they would have to find the 28,986 manuscripts (first the Greek manuscripts, then the manuscripts written during the first few centuries AD into Latin, Coptic, and Syriac).[7] After finding them, the manuscripts would need to be altered.

- Second, they would have to cross-reference the

changes that were being made, and make sure that all the manuscripts matched one another before putting them back into their place of safekeeping without anyone finding out.

Then third, after all the manuscripts in the various languages had been changed and carefully cross-referenced, someone would have to find all the writings of every person in the past who wrote anything quoting from these manuscripts. This means that the writings of the early church fathers or any other writers from the first, second, or third centuries AD would have to be found and altered, but that would be impossible. There are so many writings from the early church fathers that quote Scripture that we can reconstruct the entire New Testament from their writings alone![8] There isn't a detective squad on Earth that could find all 28,986 manuscripts and the subsequent ancient writings in order to change or destroy them.

SUPERNATURAL EVENTS

I mentioned that the Bible is filled with real people. Unlike a work of fiction, the Bible isn't filled with made-up superheroes performing amazing feats. Rather, it is filled with supernatural events performed by God. Here are some of them:

- Ten plagues were sent against Egypt so Pharoah would let God's people, the Israelites, go (Exodus 7–12).

- The waters of the Red Sea parted and stood at attention while about two million Israelites and all their livestock passed through to safety on the other side (Exodus 14).

- The sun stood still in the sky so the Israelites would have more hours to fight a battle (Joshua 10).

- A donkey actually opened its mouth and talked (Numbers 22).

- Shadrach, Meshach, and Abednego were thrown into a fiery furnace and lived to tell about it (Daniel 3)!

- Thousands were fed when Jesus multiplied two fish and five loaves of bread (Matthew 14:14-21; John 6:5-14).

- People who were born blind, deaf, mute, or lame were completely healed (Matthew 4:24; 15:30; Mark 7:37; Luke 6:19).

- Jesus walked on water, and Peter, as human as you or me, did the same (Matthew 14:22-31).

- People were resurrected from the dead. Jesus Himself lay dead for three days before the Holy Spirit raised Him from the dead (1 Kings 17:17-24; 2 Kings 4:18-35; 13:20-21; Matthew 27:50-54; Luke 7:11-17; 8:49-56; John 11:38-44; Acts 9:36-42; 20:7-12; Romans 8:11).

The Bible is the only religious text filled with supernatural events that took place in fulfillment of prophecies that were given hundreds or even thousands of years in advance. The Spirit of God literally "downloaded" these events into the authors of the Bible. Many of these authors didn't get to see the fulfillment of the prophecies that they were given.

AMAZING FACTS

In my book *The Time of Jacob's Trouble*, I said that more than 27 percent of the Bible is prophecy. Here are the details:

- there are 1,239 prophecies in the Old Testament

- there are 578 prophecies in the New Testament

- 500 of these prophecies have already been fulfilled

- all 500 have been fulfilled with 100 percent accuracy
- there are 333 prophecies concerning Jesus
- 109 of the 333 prophecies were fulfilled by Jesus' birth, life, and resurrection
- all of them were fulfilled with 100 percent accuracy
- the rest of the prophecies about Jesus will be fulfilled at His second coming

These are amazing facts! If 500 of the Bible's prophecies have already been fulfilled with 100 percent accuracy, then that should ease any doubt about the remaining prophecies being fulfilled with 100 percent accuracy. God has already carried out His promises 500 times, and He will continue to do so until every single Bible prophecy is fulfilled.[9] Again, there is no other ancient or modern religious text that contains perfectly fulfilled prophecies.

Many people reject the Bible outright, but Psalm 33:4 reminds us, "The word of the LORD holds true, and we can trust everything he does." I would imagine that many who don't trust the Bible have not read it, and that many are reluctant to trust it because it has been used as a weapon against them. God never intended for His Word to be misused against us; it is a love letter from Him to show us the way to Him.

If you're still not convinced that the Bible is the infallible and inspired Word of God, keep asking Him to help and lead you. The Bible says that His Word is a lamp to guide our feet (Psalm 119:105). "External proofs will not totally persuade. Only the Holy Spirit totally persuades."[10] Ask the Holy Spirit for enough light to take the next step of belief.

THE HOLY SPIRIT WILL TEACH YOU

A survey from 2021 revealed that only 11 percent of Americans read their Bible daily.[11] When someone is not actively in God's Word (according to this survey, it seems that 89 percent of Americans have little interest in God's Word), it is easy to be led down rabbit trails and to fall for teaching that misleads or even deceives us. Jim Cymbala said, "But even when teachers do their best, the only way for us to be ultimately blessed by the Word is through the inner teaching of the Holy Spirit. The Spirit is faithful to help us know truth from error and keep us from satanic distortions. But for all of that to happen, we must come with humble, teachable hearts."[12]

The apostle John said,

> I am writing these things to warn you about those who want to lead you astray. But you have received the Holy Spirit, and he lives within you, so you don't need anyone to teach

you what is true. For the Spirit teaches you everything you need to know, and what he teaches is true—it is not a lie. So just as he has taught you, remain in fellowship with Christ (1 John 2:26-27).

Did you catch that? When you receive Jesus as your Lord and Savior, the Holy Spirit abides in you so that you have no need that anyone should teach you—if the Holy Spirit dwells within you, you have all the teacher you need! This doesn't mean we shouldn't sit under the teaching of trustworthy Bible teachers. But it does mean the Holy Spirit is our ultimate guide, and He can help us to discern right teaching from wrong.

The Bible is the holy, divine Word of God, and the Holy Spirit teaches it to those who belong to God. It is wonderful to have the Helper, the Spirit of truth (John 15:26), who can instruct us in the classroom of our heart. It is the teaching of the Holy Spirit that opens the eyes of our hearts and enables us to understand spiritual truths (1 Corinthians 2:12-13). That is the ministry of the Holy Spirit as our teacher!

WHAT DOES IT MEAN FOR ME?

I encourage you to read the Bible daily. Don't just skim over the words, reading them as quickly as you can, but meditate on them. An online search of the word *meditate* will result in page after page of different meditation techniques, articles from psychologists, and the websites of meditation centers. None of the results in my online search included the Bible, which actually includes the word "meditating" as early as Genesis 24:63 (6,000 years ago), and says that Isaac went out into the fields to meditate. The Old Testament Hebrew meaning of the word here is to "muse pensively." To meditate on Scripture is to muse over it, ponder and study it, give it focused thought and prayer. It isn't speed-reading to see how many verses or chapters you can cover in so much time. In a Sunday morning message at Brooklyn Tabernacle, Pastor Jim Cymbala said, "You have to meditate on Bible verses. Meditate means you have to chew on it. Think about it. Talk to it. Let it talk back to you. I want to ask, 'who, what, why, when, where, how much, how long,' those kind of questions."[13]

After the death of Moses, the Lord said to Joshua, the new leader of the Israelites, "Keep this Book of the Law always on your lips; meditate on it day and night, so that you may be careful to do everything written in it. Then you will be prosperous and successful" (Joshua 1:8 NIV).

The Bible says to meditate on the Word "day and night," do what is "written in it," and "then you will be prosperous and successful." This isn't New Age jargon or something from a self-help book. God's Word says this!

The word "prosperous" in this verse means "to push forward, make progress, and break out." The word "successful" means "to wisely understand, to be circumspect and have insight."

If you are stuck in a situation and don't know or see the way out, then pick up God's Word and meditate on it. Search online for Bible verses about wisdom, hope, peace, hopelessness, anger, jealousy, anxiety, lust, bitterness, or whatever is affecting you. When you find the relevant Bible verses, open your Bible and meditate on and pray through those verses. Don't be in a hurry. Think about how those verses speak to your heart and to your situation, and you'll be "prosperous" (make progress and push forward) and "successful" (have wisdom and insight) as you do. Ask for God's peace, comfort, mercy, or hope to fill you.

If you need faith, then ask for it! James 4:2 says that we don't have because we don't ask God. If you don't like to read (but I am assuming that you do because you're reading this book), then there are many great audio Bibles to listen to on your phone. My nearly 88-year-old mother can no longer see to read, but she has the Wonder Bible, which she is able to listen to and loves it! Your faith will increase as you read or listen to the Word. As the Bible says, "Faith comes by hearing, and hearing by the word of God" (Romans 10:17 NKJV). Faith comes by listening to the Word of God! As you read or listen to God's Word and meditate on it, ponder its passages and let them move from your mind to your heart. When God's Word moves from head knowledge to heart knowledge, that is when transformation begins.

Jesus said, "Remain in my love. When you obey my commandments, you remain in my love, just as I obey my Father's commandments and remain in his love" (John 15:10). Part of the definition for "remain" in this verse is "to remain, lodge, sojourn, dwell."[14] This promise is made to those who receive Christ as their Savior: If you lodge in God's Word by reading it, if you sojourn and dwell there by meditating on it and abide in His love, the joy of Jesus will be inside of you, and your joy will be full! (John 15:11).

SEVEN

Looking at God's Timing

*I*n *Looking for Christmas*, I delve into the moment of history in which Jesus arrived. As I mentioned earlier, He came at the perfect time (Galatians 4:4), and I encourage you to read *Looking for Christmas* to discover how God put everything in place for the arrival of Jesus and His message. All through the Old Testament, we read the gradual revelations of the Jewish prophets, who, as time went on, offered more and more details that would help people to recognize the long-awaited Messiah. Had Jesus come earlier, few would have identified Him, given what little information they had.

IMPROBABLE AND REMARKABLE

There are more than 300 Old Testament prophecies about Jesus; 108 of them were fulfilled in Jesus' birth and ministry on Earth, and the rest will be fulfilled at His second coming. Moses, Micah, Zechariah, Hosea, Isaiah, the psalmists, Jeremiah, Daniel, and Malachi all prophesied about Him. Approximately 1,000 years before Christ's birth, Psalm 22:16-18 foretold that His hands and feet would be pierced, long before crucifixion was a method of execution. During Jesus' lifetime, the method used by the Jewish people was stoning, but Jesus was killed by the Romans, who used crucifixion. By the time the Jewish prophets had completed their description of the coming Savior, it was simply a matter of waiting and watching for His arrival.

Peter Stoner, author of *Science Speaks*, was the chairman of the mathematics and astronomy departments at Pasadena City College in California until 1953, when he moved to Westmont College in Santa Barbara, California, where he served as chairman of the science division. In his book, Stoner selected eight of the best-known prophecies about the Messiah and calculated the odds of their accidental fulfillment in one person as being 1 in 10^{17}. He illustrated this by asking the reader to imagine the state of Texas covered knee-deep in silver dollars. One of those silver dollars had a black check mark on it. Imagine sending a blindfolded person to walk around in that sea of silver dollars. What are the odds that the first coin he picked up would be the one with the check mark? The same as the odds of eight prophecies being fulfilled accidentally by one person.

In presenting these statistics, Stoner was stating that

when people say that the fulfillment of prophecy in Jesus' life was accidental, they do not realize how improbable that truly is! Remember, Jesus did not just fulfill eight prophecies, but 108! Stoner calculated that the chances of fulfilling 16 is 1 in 10^{45}. To fulfill 48 is to increase the odds to 1 in 10^{157}. This tells us how virtually impossible it is for these prophecies to have been fulfilled by accident![1] Jesus' fulfillment of these prophecies is remarkable.

PLEASED TO REVEAL THE SON

God's timing for sending Jesus to Earth was perfect, just as it was for when He reached the heart of the apostle Paul, and just as His timing was or will be perfect in reaching your heart. In Acts 6–9, we are introduced to Paul. He was not a good guy. He ravaged the church, dragging Christian men and women away from their homes and throwing them into prison. He heartily agreed to put Stephen, a follower of Jesus, to death, and even stood by and watched it happen. He breathed out threats and murder against the disciples of the Lord, and his primary goal in life was obvious: destroy Jesus' followers.

But in Acts 9, on his way to Damascus, Paul is blinded by a light from heaven, and a voice says, "Saul! Saul! Why are you persecuting me?" (Acts 9:4—by the way, Saul and Paul are the same person. Saul was his Hebrew name, and Paul was his Greek name).

It was Jesus who asked that question in verse 5 because when the church is persecuted, Jesus is persecuted because Jesus embodies the church. The text says that the men traveling with Paul heard the voice, but they saw no one. Because Paul had been blinded, the men had to lead him into Damascus. These men did not know Jesus, but they were being used by God to lead Paul to the home of Ananias (this is a sweet reminder that God can even use unbelievers in His plan to bring a loved one to Jesus). Ananias prayed that Paul would regain his sight and be filled with the Holy Spirit. Paul could then see again, and he would no longer be an angel of death for Christians, but an apostle of Jesus Christ.

It is interesting to read about the timing of Paul's salvation. He says, "When He who had set me apart even from my mother's womb and called me through His grace was *pleased to reveal His Son in me* so that I might preach Him among the Gentiles, I did not immediately consult with flesh and blood" (Galatians 1:15-16 NASB, emphasis added). Paul said that he came to know Jesus as Lord *when it pleased God* to reveal His Son. Just as Jesus fulfilled prophecy and came at the right time, Paul came to know Jesus at the right time. In Acts 9:15, God says, "Saul is my chosen instrument to take my message to the Gentiles and to kings, as well as to the people of Israel." God had a plan and a purpose for Paul, and it did not please Him to save

Paul any sooner than He did. If this is true of Paul, then it is true of you and me. If you are a Christian, it is true of the lost son or daughter that you are worried about. It is true of your lost spouse or parent, your best friend or grandmother.

God orchestrated the timing of Jesus' arrival on Earth. He orchestrated Paul's salvation. Paul could have gotten bogged down with the regrets of living a murderous life, but he gave his past to Jesus and accepted abundant life in Him (John 10:10). Don't let the mistakes and regrets of your past convince you that God does not have a plan or purpose for you. I'll remind you again: He does have a purpose for you, and He will fulfill that purpose (Psalm 138:8 ESV). He does not want anyone to be destroyed, but wants everyone to come to repentance (2 Peter 3:9).

If you do not yet know Jesus as Lord, then pray and ask God to give you the Spirit of wisdom and revelation in the knowledge of Him (Ephesians 1:17 ESV). Ask God to remove the scales from your eyes and reveal His Son to you.

WORDS MATTER

My husband, Troy, is a woodworker. We even make our own timber butter to use on the handcrafted furniture and charcuterie and cutting boards that he and our daughter Gracie make. We recently made some timber butter, and I used it on our wooden cabinets in the kitchen to bring out the shine. Troy came into the kitchen, picked up the tin of timber butter, and looked at the cabinets. "I think we finally found something you're good at!"

I paused for a second. "*Finally* found something I'm good at? As if I've been floundering up to this point? Making timber butter is what I'm *finally* good at?"

He started to laugh and said, "That's not what I mean. You're putting the emphasis on the wrong word." He then spent the next minute or so putting the emphasis on *think, found, something, you're,* and *good.* We both laughed hysterically because there wasn't a good way to say that sentence at all! Words are important. They carry weight.

Jesus came from the Father to do the Father's work (Luke 2:49). With Jesus on Earth, the kingdom of heaven was at hand. When He began His public ministry, the first words He said were, "Repent of your sins and turn to God, for the Kingdom of Heaven is near" (Matthew 4:17). His first word was "repent." The dictionary definition is "to feel pain, sorrow, or regret, for what one has done or omitted to do." Despite what today's culture says, Jesus' attitude was not one of "Just do what works for you." Any parent who truly loves their child does not let them just do "what works for you." A good parent sets boundaries. Repentance from our sins is so important that it is the first thing that Jesus spoke about when He began His ministry. He didn't tell us to follow our own truth; rather, He said that He was the truth and to follow Him (John 8:31-32; 10:27; 14:6; 17:17).

Our words matter in this "do what works for you" world. My pastor, Darren Tyler, said,

> If you are in Christ, every sin that you have committed, are committing, or will commit, will be forgiven of you. That is what Jesus did on the cross. But if you make that sin your identity—"That's just who I am. It's how I'm made"—you put the white flag of surrender up because you are no longer struggling. You have given in to that sin and ignored the Paraclete, the Holy Spirit. If you are struggling with any sin that is becoming your identity, I encourage you to keep the fight going, do not wave the white flag. It is not who you are.[2]

Jesus came to bring us life in abundance and to set us free from slavery to sin, but that only happens when we repent before Him (2 Chronicles 7:14; Proverbs 28:13; Acts 3:19; 1 John 1:9).

One day, when Jesus was with His apostles, He asked them, "Who do the people say that the Son of Man is?" They told Him that some thought He was one of the prophets or maybe John the Baptist, and He asked them, "But who do you say I am?" (Matthew 16:13-17). That question is still relevant today. Who do *you* say that Jesus is? Scottish preacher "Rabbi" John Duncan (1796–1870) made up the word *trilemma* when he said, "Christ either deceived mankind by conscious fraud, or He was Himself deluded and self-deceived, or He was Divine. There is no getting out of this trilemma."[3] C.S. Lewis (1898–1963) popularized the saying that Jesus was either a liar, a lunatic, or the Lord.

"I am the way, the truth, and the life. No one can come to the Father except through me" (John 14:6). Jesus was either a liar or a lunatic when He said that, or He was who He said He was—Lord—the Savior whom you need who will give you the real love you need in an unreal world. In a survey, a whopping 52 percent of those who call themselves Christians believe in a works-oriented way to God.[4] But God's Word says it is our faith in Jesus, not our works, that make us right before Him (Romans 3:28). The gospel message is that the death and resurrection of Jesus atones for our sin and makes us a new creation in Christ (1 Corinthians 15:1-5; 2 Corinthians 5:17). Somehow, many have replaced the gospel message with works and have managed to take our sin and the reason for the cross out of it. According to this recent poll, the majority of those who profess to be Christians believe the cross isn't necessary for salvation.

We can easily design a Jesus and salvation that we want ("Just do what works for you," or "Follow your personal truth"), but that is not the Savior that we need. We can't pick and choose the scriptures about Him that we want to keep and discard the ones that make us cringe. We can't put words into His mouth. We can't create a different Jesus, or a different Spirit, or different gospel (2 Corinthians 11:4) to suit our needs. The Jesus that we *want* would not say to us, "Repent." But the Savior that we *need* does say "Repent" to us, because He knows it is only through repentance that we come to the Father.

THE KINGDOM OF HEAVEN IS AT HAND

The book of Luke includes an account from the beginning of Jesus' ministry in which words are also important. Jesus had gone to Nazareth (where He grew up) and entered a synagogue. A scroll of Isaiah was handed to Him, and He began to read.

> "The Spirit of the LORD is upon me, for he has anointed me to bring Good News to the poor. He has sent me to proclaim that captives will be released, that the blind will see, that the oppressed will be set free, and that the time of the LORD's favor has come."
>
> He rolled up the scroll, handed it back to the attendant, and sat down. All eyes in the synagogue looked at him intently. Then he began to speak to them. "The Scripture you've just

heard has been fulfilled this very day!" (Luke 4:18-21).

The portion of the scroll that Jesus read from is found in Isaiah chapter 61. But the passage Jesus quoted in Isaiah 61 doesn't end with the words "the LORD's favor has come." It ends with "and the day of vengeance of our God" (verse 2 NKJV).

In the synagogue, Jesus stopped reading at a comma. Why would He do that? Nobody stops reading at a comma! He stopped because when Jesus walked the earth, it wasn't time yet for the day of the Lord's vengeance. That day is in the future. He stopped at the comma because His ministry was about proclaiming the good news— "The kingdom of heaven is at hand!" His ministry was about proclaiming liberty to the captives, those who were enslaved by sin and living in darkness. He had come to heal the blind and the sick and to set free all those who were oppressed. Jesus came that we would have the Lord's favor of abundant life! Now is the time—this is the time of the comma—to take to heart the words of Jesus and believe on Him. This is the time of His mercy and grace and abundant life and love. He wants you to know that love today.

OVERWHELMED AND TOTALLY AMAZED

In Roman census returns from the first to third

centuries, it is revealed that the average lifespan was around 22 to 25 years old.[5] The main cause of death was said to be infections, whether from infectious diseases or from wounds from accidents or fighting. Researchers were able to come to this young average age of death by examining skeletons inside tombs. Back then, tombs were owned by the rich and those who could afford medical care, medicines, and treatment. A look inside their tombs revealed that the skeletons were often of children or young people, bringing researchers to the conclusion that the average lifespan was about 25 years of age. If the rich, who could afford doctors and medications, were dying young, how much younger were the poor dying? With that in mind, it makes perfect sense why large crowds would follow Jesus. He could heal! There is no other religious figure in history who has been able to do this.

We are told that at the beginning of Jesus' ministry, He "traveled throughout the region of Galilee, teaching in the synagogues and announcing the Good News about the Kingdom. And he healed every kind of disease and illness" (Matthew 4:23). "Many believed in His name, when they saw the miracles which he did" (John 2:23 KJV).

One day, a large crowd was around Jesus when one of the rulers at a synagogue ran to Him and fell at His feet. Men, especially men of prominence at that time, did not run, and they absolutely did not fall at the feet of another man, but this man was desperate. His daughter was dying. He begged Jesus earnestly and said, "My little daughter is dying…Please come and lay your hands on her; heal her so she can live" (Mark 5:23). This man would certainly be able to afford doctors and medication, but because he pleaded with Jesus, we can assume that doctors were not helping the girl. Some people from his home found him and told him not to bother Jesus because his daughter had already died, but Jesus looked at him and said, "Do not be afraid; only believe" (Mark 5:36 NKJV).

In keeping with this chapter's theme that words are important, when Jesus and the father finally arrived at the home, Jesus spoke words to the mourners who had already gathered and were weeping and wailing. He said, "The child isn't dead; she's only asleep" (verse 39). This same One who was talking to them spoke the world into existence, but they didn't believe His words. They began to laugh and scoff, and Jesus put them outside the house. Although many believed in Jesus and what He could do, most did not. "Despite all the miraculous signs Jesus had done, *most of the people still did not believe in him*" (John 12:37, emphasis added). The mourners at this little girl's house fell into this camp; they did not believe.

After Jesus put them outside, He took Peter, James, John, and the girl's parents into the room where she was laying. We can picture Him sitting on the side of the bed and gently speaking these words to her: "Little girl, get up!" (Mark 5:41). Immediately she got up and walked around! She was raised from the dead, and the Bible says that Peter, James, John, and the girl's parents "were overwhelmed and totally amazed" (verse 42).

I want to be overwhelmed and totally amazed as I walk with Jesus. I don't want to pick and choose the words that He said to suit me, but to believe every word that He said. I don't want to cobble together a savior that I want, but I want to claim and follow the Savior I need.

Everybody who laughed and scoffed at Jesus' words that day—those who were sent outside the house, those who did not believe that "the kingdom of heaven is at hand"—missed it. They missed the miracle! They missed walking with Jesus as He ministered to these grieving parents and returned their joy to them.

WHO GOES THERE?

In old war movies or spy thrillers, there is often a scene in which a guard is posted at a door. When someone knocks, the guard will say, "Who goes there?" The name of the person on the other side of the door or the recognition of a familiar voice will gain their entrance.

The world was noisy enough when Jesus was born, but there are a lot more voices around us today. Between phones, the internet, radios, and television, we could be bombarded into oblivion with voices. Whose voice are you listening to? Who are you believing?

In John 10:3-5, Jesus talked about sheep, and the Bible describes the followers of Jesus as sheep. He said,

> The gatekeeper opens the gate for him, and the sheep recognize his voice and come to him. He calls his own sheep by name and leads them out. After he has gathered his own flock, he walks ahead of them, and they follow him because they know his voice. They won't follow a stranger; they will run from him because they don't know his voice.

Online, it is fascinating and fun to watch sheep responding to their shepherd's voice. When they hear their shepherd speak, they will separate from an entire flock (where they don't belong) and run to their shepherd. Those who know the Good Shepherd know His voice, and recognize when He is trying to get their attention (they may not always respond, but they know who He is).

Shepherds watch over and protect their flocks; they lead them away from danger to safety. They lead them to food and water and a place to rest. In the same way, we can know that Jesus is the Good Shepherd and will lead us and protect us; He won't harm us. Just like sheep trust their shepherd in the field, we can trust the Good Shepherd because we know who He is. John 10:14 says, "I am the good shepherd; I know my own sheep, and they know me."

Our own family members can misunderstand us, but Jesus knows us. He knows everything about us (Psalm 139:1). He knows everything we do (verse 3). He knows the next word we will speak (verse 4). He even knows the number of hairs on our head (Luke 12:7). We may have to explain ourselves to others, but we never have to explain ourselves to Jesus because He knows everything there is to know about us.

Jesus' sheep know that as the Lamb of God, He came to give His life for them. He says in John 10:28, "I give them eternal life, and they will never perish. No one can snatch them away from me."

Sheep wander and put themselves in danger. I saw one shepherd online retrieve one of his sheep from a deep hole, and as soon as the sheep was out and free, it jumped right back into the hole again!

Sheep are dumb. Our longtime friends Bob and Dannah Gresh own a hobby farm in Pennsylvania. While we were visiting them in August 2022, we met the newest member of the farm, a cute little black sheep named Epley. He was still being bottle-fed, and on our first day there, my daughter Kate and I went out to help feed him. Kate held onto the bottle and a goat inside the barn readily recognized what Kate was carrying and came running, thinking that he could enjoy some of Epley's delicious milk. Epley came running too (probably because he saw the goat running toward us), but when he saw the bottle, he didn't know what to do, and he had been doing this same routine for weeks!

"He's not very bright," Dannah said. "You will have to put it up to his mouth." Kate and I started to laugh at this poor, confused, but adorable little sheep. "It's not a compliment when we are called sheep in the Bible," Dannah said, shaking her head and laughing. Sheep make the same mistakes over and over again, but the shepherd is there to rescue them, lead them, and feed them. If you are in Christ, if you follow Him as your Shepherd, you will never perish. No one and no thing will be able to snatch you out of His hand. You are one of His beloved sheep, and He will watch over and tenderly care for you.

STAY NEAR THE GOOD SHEPHERD

As I was writing this chapter, Cathy Sorenson, one of the women from our church prayer group, texted me this quote from A.W. Tozer. The timing of the text was perfect for this chapter: "Your spiritual safety and well-being lies in being near to the Shepherd. Stay close to Jesus and all of the wolves in the world cannot get a tooth in you." Wolves of this world are always attacking, so as followers of Jesus, we must stay close to our Good Shepherd.

Jesus cared for and led His flock out of His love and compassion for them as the Good Shepherd. So you can imagine the distress of His sheep when He told them that He would be leaving them soon (John 13:33). He knew His death was near. By this time, He had been teaching the disciples for three years. What if the sheep forgot what they had heard or what they had seen Him do? How could they do all that He had taught them when He was no longer there to show them the way? They had so many questions and there was much they did not understand. How would they carry on or hear the Shepherd's voice?

Jesus said to them, "I will pray the Father, and he will give you another *Helper*, that He may abide with you forever...the *Helper*, the Holy Spirit, whom the Father will send in My name, He will teach you all things, and bring to your remembrance all things that I said to you" (John 14:16, 26 NKJV, emphasis added). His sheep would continue to hear His voice through the Holy Spirit within them. They would not be left alone in this world.

If you are in Christ, you are not alone. He has promised to be with you always, even to the very end of the age (Matthew 28:20). His love for you never ends.

EIGHT

Final Thoughts in a Noisy World

Several years ago, I asked our pastor's wife if I could start a prayer group for women that would meet one morning a week. We started off small, with only three or four of us getting together, and have grown into a group of 30 plus. Not all of us can meet each week, but we all can pray for the various needs of our church, community, and world.

One morning, I pulled into the parking lot early, and Debbie Sayovitz, a recent California transplant who had moved here with her husband Mike to be closer to their kids and grandkids, was getting out of her car. Two young women were waiting nearby in their car and got out when they saw us. One of the women was coming in for prayer, and the look on her face was of total anguish. Her knees began to buckle, and Debbie and I ran to support her. I quickly realized that in her frame of mind, it would not be in her best interest to have 15 or more women gathered around praying for her. That could make her feel awkward. I thought privacy would be best and saw that one of the church offices was open, so we led her and her friend in there, then closed the door.

She immediately began yelling. Yes, yelling. "God doesn't love me! God doesn't love me!"

"He does love you," Debbie and I both assured her.

"But I can't do anything right," she screamed. She was in a manic state and dug her fingers into her face. "There's nothing that I can do to make Him love me!"

"That's right," Debbie said in a calm voice. "You can't do anything to make God love you because He already loves you!"

"No! No! No!" She continued yelling. "He doesn't love me!"

We asked if she was a true believer in Christ, and she was confident of her salvation. I said, "All who are in Christ have the Holy Spirit living inside of us. He testifies to you of God's love for you! He reassures you of God's presence and love in your life."

She looked at me and Debbie with her face scrunched up in pain. "But I can't feel Him! I can't hear Him in my life!"

Nor could she hear anything that Debbie and I said. In this noisy world where the wolves were attacking, she could not sense or hear God in her life. The only message she could hear from this world was that God did not love her, and He could not possibly love her because she could not do anything right.

TORN AND PULLED

We live in a chaotic and distracting world where the wolves are fierce around us. Simply by picking up our cell phones, we can have hours of distractions at our fingertips. We can enter into a world of games, news, streaming services, or the rabbit hole that is social media, and before we know it, the day is gone, and we have given little thought to the One who loves us more than we can imagine. And despite living in one of the wealthiest nations in the world with every pleasure literally within reach, depression and anxiety are on the rise. Suicides hit an all-time high in 2022 and are more common than at any time since the dawn of WWII.[1] Anxiety disorders affect 42.5 million adults in America, and 21 million live with depression.[2] Today, one out of eight people live with a mental health condition. That's nearly one billion people worldwide.[3] The young woman who came in for prayer that morning falls into these statistics, and ended up under medical supervision. She said she could not hear God or feel Him. She didn't even know her identity as God's child anymore. Deception sets in when we make the focus of our identity anything but God. That can easily happen in a world of chaos and confusion.

Our culture rages at us through wolves on social media, the news, in the halls of education and in government, and even inside many of our churches, perverting who God says we are, twisting His Word and drowning out His voice. As I mentioned earlier, if you feel deep inside of you that you are seeking something greater than the uproar of this world, it is because God has set eternity in your heart (Ecclesiastes 3:11). The Holy Spirit is nudging you to shut out the distractions and seek the God who loves you and created you. He gave His Son for you so you could live in eternity with Him. "This is how God loved the world: He gave his one and only Son, so that everyone who believes in him will not perish but have eternal life" (John 3:16).

When we receive the invitation from the Spirit to put our foundation in Jesus, we make Him the focus of our lives and stop striving to be our own savior. When we no longer feel the need to fight for self-worth, but rest in our identity in Him, we willingly obey what His Word says. Jesus said that those who obey, abide in, and keep His Word love Him and are truly His disciples (John 8:31; 14:15, 21, 23-24; 15:10-15; 1 John 3:24). Mary, the mother of Jesus, did not boast in or lift herself up to be equal with Jesus, but rather, she pointed to the Son. She said, "Do whatever he tells you" (John 2:5). Her words echo through the ages to us today.

Jesus is the Word (John 1:1-5, 14). Do whatever the Word tells you.

WHICH WOLF ARE YOU FEEDING?

A story is often told of a grandfather talking to his grandson about right and wrong. "There are two wolves fighting inside you," the grandfather said. "One wants you to do what is right, but the other wants you to do what is wrong."

"Which one wins?" his grandson asked.

"The one you feed," the grandfather said.

Are you filling up your spirit with the candy that the world offers, or are you feeding upon the living bread of heaven? The Spirit of God gently nudges us, prodding us to do the right thing and to seek God. But if we say no and do things our own way, we end up pushing Him out of our lives. When we ignore the Holy Spirit's efforts to engage us, we will fall for any deception that this world throws at us. Jesus said, "When the Spirit of truth comes, he will guide you into all truth. He will not speak on his own but will tell you what he has heard" (John 16:13). If we leave guidance to ourselves and to culture, we will be confused and frustrated, caught up in what my friend Carmen called at the beginning of this book "an endless cycle of folly."

God's Word is alive. It didn't die or end when the final word was written in the last book of the Bible, Revelation.

God's Word is alive and active now speaking to you. He says in 2 Corinthians 6:2, "Indeed, the 'right time' is now. Today is the day of salvation." In whatever condition you find yourself living, through whatever racket that is clanging in your life, God still has a plan for you. He wants you back. He wants you to live in eternity with Him. When you look for Him wholeheartedly, you will find Him (Jeremiah 29:13). That is a real promise from God in an unreal world.

WHAT SHOULD YOU DO WITH JESUS?

The Irish poet Nick Laird wrote, "Time is how you spend your love."[4] Throughout time, God has spent His love on us. I hope that as you have read this book, you have felt His real love for you. When Jesus stood before Pontius Pilate, the governor of Judea, Pilate asked the crowd, "What should I do with Jesus who is called the Messiah?" (Matthew 27:22). That question is the most important one you will ever answer. What should you do with Jesus?

Two angels asked an equally powerful question to a group of women who, after the crucifixion, went to Jesus' tomb and were shocked to find it empty (Luke 24:1-3). The angels asked them, "Why are you looking among the dead for someone who is alive?" (verse 5).

When we treat Jesus as simply a prophet, an idea, a good moral person, or the head of a religious movement, we are looking among the dead for someone who is alive. That Jesus is as dead as if he were Buddha or Muhammad, whose graves are not empty, but rather, full of their bones. Seeking those who are dead will not bring us life.

Jesus' grave is empty because He is alive and seated at the right hand of the Father (Acts 2:33; Romans 8:34). When we seek Jesus as a living person, we encounter Him for who He is—our risen, living Savior. This real, living Savior can give you the peace, wisdom, strength, and real love you need in an unreal world. Only then will the seeds that have been planted in your life *about* Jesus grow into a transformative relationship *with* Him.

If this is the beginning or continuation of your search for God, I pray that you will feel His presence and you will ask Jesus to be the Savior of your life. If you don't know Jesus as your Savior but want to, I encourage you to pray this simple prayer:

> *Dear Jesus,*
>
> *Thank You for loving me so much that You came from heaven to Earth for me. Thank You for salvation in Your name alone! I repent of my sins today and declare that You are Lord! I want You to be the Savior of my life and teach me Your ways. Your Word says that everyone who calls on the name of the Lord will be saved, so thank You for saving me today!*

If you prayed this from a sincere heart, you have received the greatest gift in life—salvation in Christ—and the Helper (John 15:26), the Holy Spirit, has now come to live within you. As you walk with Him, you will learn how to hear His voice and recognize His gentle nudges as He guides you. If you are not part of a gospel-teaching church, please find one that unashamedly teaches the gospel of Jesus Christ. Your new friends there will help lead you deeper into the Word of God and into a more intimate relationship with Him.

As you begin your walk with God and get into His Word, I pray that you will realize how much you are loved. I do hope we can meet each other again! Until next time,

> The LORD bless you
>   and keep you;
>   the LORD make his face shine on you
>   and be gracious to you;
>   the LORD turn his face toward you
>   and give you peace (Numbers 6:24-26 NIV).

Notes

CHAPTER 1—LOOKING AT GOD'S HEART FOR YOU

1. Bruce Marshall, *The World, the Flesh and Father Smith* (Boston, MA: Houghton Mifflin, 1945), 108.

2. A.W. Tozer, *The Essential Tozer Collection*, compiled and edited by James L. Snyder (Minneapolis, MN: Bethany House, 2002), 26-27.

3. Henri Nouwen, "We Are Seen by God's Loving Eyes," *Henri Nouwen Society*, August 12, 2024, https://henrinouwen.org/meditations/we-are-seen-by-gods-loving-eyes/.

4. "Tom Brady on winning: There's 'got to be more than this,'" *60 Minutes*, https://www.youtube.com/watch?v=-TA4_fVkv3c&list=PLI1yx5Z0Lrv5iNi5W5vk7a0819ulTrS7n.

5. Tozer, *The Essential Tozer Collection*, 22.

6. Charles Spurgeon, *All of Grace* (Nashville, TN: B&H Publishing, 2017), 6.

7. Simon Rogers, "Year in Search 2022: All about new possibilities," *Google*, December 8, 2022, https://blog.google/products/search/year-in-search-2022-all-about-new-possibilities/.

8. "Top 100: The Most Visited Websites in the US," *Semrush Blog*, 2025, https://www.semrush.com/blog/most-visited-websites/.

9. Naveen Kumar, "How Many Google Searches Per Day [2025 Data]," *demandsage*, May 22, 2025, https://www.demandsage.com/google-search-statistics/.

10. Tozer, *The Essential Tozer Collection*, 25.

11. Spurgeon, *All of Grace*, 7.

CHAPTER 2—LOOKING AT THE GOD WHO ADOPTS YOU

1. Paul David Tripp, *Do You Believe?* (Wheaton, IL: Crossway, 2021), 269 (emphasis in original).

2. A.W. Tozer, *The Essential Tozer Collection*, compiled and edited by James L Snyder (Minneapolis, MN: Bethany House, 2009), 25.

CHAPTER 3—LOOKING AT THE CREATOR OF LOVE

1. Tim Keller, *The Reason for God* (New York: Riverhead Books, 2008), 223-224.

2. "The Oneness of Allah," *Al-Islam.org*, https://www.al-islam.org/islamic-doctrines-simplified/oneness-allah.

3. "Allah, the Best Deceiver (Qur'an 3:54)," *WikiIslam*, https://wikiislam.net/wiki/Allah,_the_Best_Deceiver_(Qur%27an_3:54).

4. "Answering Islam," *Answering-Islam.org*, https://answering-islam.org/authors/shamoun/abu_bakr_fear.html.

5. "Hadith," *Britannica*, https://www.britannica.com/topic/Hadith.

6. *Sahih al-Bukhari*, Volume 5, Book 58, Number 266.

7. Michael Reeves, *Delighting in the Trinity* (Downers Grove, IL: InterVarsity, 2012), 112.

8. Fouad Masri, *Connecting with Muslims* (Downers Grove, IL: InterVarsity, 2014), 144-145.

9. J.D. Greear, "Your God Is Too Small," *ChurchLeaders*, February 21, 2018, https://churchleaders.com/outreach-missions/outreach-missions-articles/319703-god-small-jd-greear.html.

10. Sam Wellman, *C.S. Lewis* (Uhrichsville, OH: Barbour Publishing, 1996), 109.

CHAPTER 4—LOOKING AT THE GOD WHO SEES YOU

1. Jana Harmon, "What I Learned from 100 Atheists Who Converted to Christianity," *The Worldview Bulletin Newsletter*, July 9, 2023, https://worldviewbulletin.substack.com/p/what-i-learned-from-100-atheists.

2. Russell McKinney, "The Clinched Fist of Joseph Stalin," *The Disciple's Road*, December 15, 2011, https://russellmckinney.com/2011/12/15/the-clinched-fist-of-joseph-stalin/.

CHAPTER 5—LOOKING AT OUR HELPER

1. Bethany Verrett, "What Exactly Is Our Spirit?," *Bible Study Tools*, updated June 16, 2023, https://www.biblestudytools.com/bible-study/topical-studies/what-exactly-is-our-spirit.html.

2. Peyton Jones, "In His Absence," *Christianity Today*, September 29, 2015, https://www.christianitytoday.com/2015/09/in-his-absence/.

3. "lypeō," *Blue Letter Bible*, https://www.blueletterbible.org/lexicon/g3076/kjv/tr/0-1/.

4. *Oswald Chambers: The Best from All His Books, Vol. 2*, ed. Harry Verploegh (Nashville, TN: Thomas Nelson, 1989), 138.

5. "Comforter," *Merriam-Webster.com*, https://www.merriam-webster.com/dictionary/comforter.

6. Oswald Chambers, *My Utmost for His Highest* (New York: Dodd, Mead, 1935), 102.

CHAPTER 6—LOOKING AT GOD'S WORD

1. A.W. Tozer, *The Essential Tozer Collection*, compiled and edited by James L. Snyder (Minneapolis, MN: Bethany House, 2009), 72, 73, 74, 78.

2. R.T. Kendall, *Word and Spirit* (Lake Mary, FL: Charisma House, 2019), 96.

3. Kendall, *Word and Spirit*, 15.

4. Frank Newport, "Fewer in U.S. Now See Bible as Literal Word of God," *Gallup*, July 6, 2022, https://news.gallup.com/poll/394262/fewer-bible-literal-word-god.aspx.

5. Sean McDowell, "What Is the Most Recent Manuscript Count for the New Testament?," *Sean McDowell*, March 13, 2018,

https://seanmcdowell.org/blog/what-is-the-most-recent-manuscript-count-for-the-new-testament.

6. Josh McDowell Ministry Team, "Testing the Historical Reliability of the New Testament," *Josh McDowell*, https://www.josh.org/historical-reliability-new-testament/.

7. "Where Can We Find the Biblical Manuscripts That Still Exist?," *Blue Letter Bible*, https://www.blueletterbible.org/Comm/stewart_don/faq/words-bible/question13-can-we-find-biblical-manuscripts-still-exist.cfm.

8. "The Manuscripts," *Institute for Creation Research*, https://www.icr.org/bible-manuscripts.

9. Donna VanLiere, *The Time of Jacob's Trouble* (Eugene, OR: Harvest House, 2020), 199.

10. VanLiere, *The Time of Jacob's Trouble*, 14.

11. "Frequency of reading the Bible among adults in the United States from 2018 to 2021," *statista*, https://www.statista.com/statistics/299433/bible-readership-in-the-usa/.

12. Jim Cymbala, *Spirit Rising* (Grand Rapids, MI: Zondervan, 2012), 59.

13. I documented this statement from a video by Jim Cymbala, but have since been unable to access the video.

14. "International Standard Bible Encyclopedia—Abide," *Bible Study Tools*, https://www.biblestudytools.com/dictionary/abide/.

CHAPTER 7—LOOKING AT GOD'S TIMING

1. Peter Stoner, as cited in David R. Reagan, "Applying the Science of Probability to the Scriptures," *Lamb & Lion Ministries*, https://christinprophecy.org/articles/applying-the-science-of-probability-to-the-scriptures/.

2. "Believe Series: John 16:1-15," Conduit Church, *YouTube*, https://www.youtube.com/watch?v=HdOg4CuFe3I.

3. Justin Taylor, "Is C.S. Lewis's Liar-Lord-or-Lunatic Argument Unsound?," *TGC*, February 1, 2016, https://www.thegospelcoalition

.org/blogs/justin-taylor/is-c-s-lewiss-liar-lord-or-lunatic-argument -unsound/.

4. Joe Carter, "Survey: Majority of American Christians Don't Believe the Gospel," *TGC*, August 9, 2020, https://www.thegospelcoalition.org /article/survey-a-majority-of-american-christians-dont-believe-the-gospel/.

5. "Ancient World, Demography Of," *Encyclopedia.com*, https://www .encyclopedia.com/social-sciences/encyclopedias-almanacs-transcripts -and-maps/ancient-world-demography.

CHAPTER 8—FINAL THOUGHTS IN A NOISY WORLD

1. Mike Stobbe, "US suicides hit an all-time high last year," *AP News*, updated August 10, 2023, https://apnews.com/article/suicides-record -2022-guns-48511d74deb24d933e66cec1b6f2d545.

2. Lizzie Duszynski-Goodman, "Mental Health Statistics and Facts," *Forbes*, February 21, 2024, https://www.forbes.com/health/mind/mental -health-statistics/.

3. Fred Schwaller, "Global mental health issues on the rise," *DW*, October 10, 2022, https://www.dw.com/en/mental-health-issues-like-depression-and -anxiety-on-the-rise-globally/a-63371304.

4. Nick Laird, *goodreads*, https://www.goodreads.com/quotes/11089488 -time-is-how-you-spend-your-love-from-his-poem.

Other Great Reading by Donna VanLiere

Exploring the people and places in the biblical Nativity story, Donna VanLiere invites you to a richer, more meaningful connection with what Christmas is truly about.

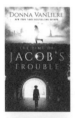

The *New York Times* bestselling novelist of *The Christmas Shoes* now explores a future world facing the final days. Donna VanLiere weaves end-times prophecies into the lives of Emma and her friends as they struggle to survive and come face-to-face with the chilling truth.

In this gripping follow-up to *The Time of Jacob's Trouble*, bestselling author Donna VanLiere explores the end-times prophecies in the journeys of Emma, Zerah, and others who cling to hope even as danger closes in and civilization crumbles on an unprecedented scale.

In this conclusion to the end-times trilogy that began with *The Time of Jacob's Trouble*, the bestselling author of *The Christmas Shoes* brings the stories of Emma and Zerah to a riveting close. In the final chapters, you'll discover what God's Word says about the glorious future that awaits you, and see that things aren't spiraling downward but are looking up!